say it with Hands

louie j. fant, jr.

Department of Education
Gallaudet College
Washington, D. C.

illustrated by

elizabeth g. miller

Department of Art
Gallaudet College
Washington, D.C.

*Much of this book was made possible through a grant from the
Vocational Rehabilitation Administration of the Department of
Health, Education and Welfare, United States Government.*

© 1964, by Louie J. Fant, Jr.
1st Printing 1964
2nd Printing 1965
3rd Printing 1966
4th Printing 1967
5th Printing 1968
6th Printing 1969
7th Printing 1969
8th Printing 1970
9th Printing 1970
10th Printing 1975
11th Printing 1976
National Association of the Deaf
814 Thayer Avenue
Silver Spring, Md. 20910

Library of Congress Catalog Card No. 65-1226

To my parents—
who taught me to see as well as to listen

FOREWORD

It is a pleasure to write a foreword for this new book illustrating the most interesting language of signs. Inquiries continue to come to the college in ever increasing numbers concerning the availability of material helpful to those interested in communicating with the deaf. Fortunately a new interest in this problem has brought out new texts. Each such effort has a unique approach to the problem that is helpful.

Professor Fant is well known as a fine interpreter. This ability is evident in this book. It should be of great help to those who are just beginning to communicate as well as those who wish to improve their use of this means of communication.

Great credit is due those who take the time to write and publish such books. The market may be small, but the need is great. This book will be happily received by all who work in this field.

Leonard M. Elstad
President
Gallaudet College

PREFACE

For many years the only book designed to help students familiarize themselves with the language of signs was the dictionary published by J. Schulyer Long in 1910. During the past five years, however, a renewed interest has manifested itself in manual communication for the deaf, and a number of books have been published on various aspects of this form of communication.

A few studies are being done at the present time in the field of linguistics as it pertains to the language of signs. Some recent studies have also been made using slides for teaching communication manually.

The number of classes in the United States in colleges and universities, schools for the deaf, parent groups, and rehabilitation centers being organized for teaching manual communication has greatly increased.

Professor Fant's approach to learning the language of signs is somewhat unique in that the book is not a dictionary, but illustrations and directions on how to teach the various symbols. The book should be of great help to house parents, teachers, rehabilitation workers, rabbis, priests, ministers, and social workers.

Professor Fant has had much experience in teaching manual communication and in interpreting for the adult deaf, especially religious groups. This book should fill a long felt need in this specialized field of communication.

Powrie V. Doctor
Editor
American Annals of the Deaf

INTRODUCTION

We are witnessing today an unprecedented boom in sign language classes springing up everywhere. The "Berlin Wall," which for so long has separated the deaf from their hearing contemporaries, is crumbling readily as society discovers a formidable tool of communication so easy and so dramatic to use in the everyday intercourse of human affairs. The tool is old, but it gains in stature, dignity and effectiveness when people with their faculties intact are skilfully instructed in the three phases of this language—colloquial, conventional and dignified platform usage.

Under the sponsorship of the United States Vocational Rehabilitation Administration, the District of Columbia Association of the Deaf has conducted classes in sign language instruction for the past two years. It has helped immensely to narrow the long standing gap between the deaf and the hearing world. These classes have also provided a testing ground for the usefulness of this book.

For many years, publications of books on sign language have been few and far between. Sign language, like any other language, is dynamic. It is constantly undergoing changes. Obsolete signs are being dropped, new ones are embraced and put into wide circulation. Those once labeled as slang, find ready modern acceptance, so the urgent need for an up-to-date manual on sign language in both illustrated and written form is underlined. Several dictionaries on dactylology have recently appeared on the market, but so far few have been prepared for classroom instructional purposes.

Now comes Louie J. Fant, Jr. into the picture. As professor in the teacher training department of Gallaudet College, he devoted many hours to the task of perfecting a manual expressly for classroom use. It is the first book of its kind to come off the press and is receiving acclaim from many influential quarters. An early acquaintance with this book will convince the possessor that it just meets the need of the hour.

David Peikoff, General Chairman
Gallaudet College Centennial Fund
Commission

Washington, D.C.
January, 1964

SOME COMMENTS ON
MANUAL COMMUNICATION

The subject of this book is sign language. The purpose is to provide an introduction to the system of manual communication used by almost all adult deaf people in the United States. Although the title of this book focuses attention on the hands, much more is involved than merely the movement of the hands.

In ordinary conversation, deaf people use formal signs, finger spelling, pantomime gestures, facial expressions, body movements and speech to convey meaning. All of these must be part of the student's introduction to manual communication, and they obviously spill over the confining limits of *sign language.*

Estimates have placed the number of formal signs variously from fifteen hundred to two thousand. Though this may appear to the student as a formidable number of signs to master, it is actually very small considering the vast number of ideas to be expressed. In this book, only some 500 signs will be taught. These are basic and will provide a foundation upon which to build.

A very critical skill which the student must develop is the ability to evaluate a deaf person's educational and cultural level. This enables him to sense whether he is getting through to the deaf person. The language handicap and cultural restriction which deafness imposes frustrate communication far more than the inability to sign clearly or finger spell fluently. The lessons attempt to teach the student to gear the conversation to the level of the deaf person.

Many professional workers with deaf people have observed that as deaf people move up the ladder of educational achievement and broaden their social and cultural horizons, they tend to use fewer signs and more finger spelling. Conversely as they move down the ladder, and their experiences are far more restricted, then the signs increase, and finger spelling decreases. (The reason for this will be discussed later.) If the student observes the deaf person using more or fewer signs, he has one measure by which to gauge that person's level and he can adjust his communication accordingly.

Though this book will help the student learn a great deal on his own, he will still need the help of someone who is fluent in manual communication. This is particularly important for providing the student with practice in receiving communication. Needless to say, the more the student associates with deaf people, the more adept he becomes in manual communication.

A sign represents a concept. It may also, but not necessarily, represent an English word. When one makes the sign for "no," it represents the concept of prohibitiveness as well as the word *no*. However, when one makes the sign for "tired," it represents the concept of tiredness, but it may be represented by such English words as *weary, fatigued, all-in, exhausted*, etc.

The question of how deaf people think has not yet been adequately researched. However, many professional workers believe that deaf people make no attempt to "translate" signs into English words. Their minds comprehend that the concept *tiredness*, for example, is intended by the sign for "tired," and this is sufficient for their understanding. The student must learn to accept the concept and not try to find an English word for it. Use signs that will express the concept, do not choose signs on the basis of the English word you have in mind.

An example of the misunderstanding that can take place occurs in the word *take*. There are many concepts represented by this one English word. We *take* a letter to the Post Office (carry); we *take* medicine (swallow); we *take* courses in college (study, register, attend); we *take* sick (contract, catch); and so on. Each of these concepts has a different sign. Consider the illogicalness of the sentence, "I will take the bitter pill of experience," when *take* is signed "carry." In other words, just because the English word *take* is used to express these various concepts is no reason to use a simple sign to express all of them. Quite the opposite is true.

If it is important to know the precise English word intended, then finger spelling must be used. This is why the better educated deaf person with rich cultural experiences prefers to use more finger spelling than signs. He appreciates the importance of words and their fine shades of meaning. He has overcome his language handicap whereas those deaf people on the lower rungs of the ladder have not. For them the general concept is sufficient. They do not care if the person was *fatigued* or *exhausted*, just the fact that he was *tired* is adequate. This is due to their language handicap, not to lack of intelligence or ambition.

Finger Spelling

Each letter of the alphabet can be represented by a configuration of the fingers. In the United States we use only the fingers of one hand while in some countries, the fingers of both hands are used.

Finger spelling is nothing more or less than English spelled on the fingers. It has great merit for teaching English to deaf children. Signs, you will recall, do not necessarily represent words, but concepts. Since a verb sign such as "go" represents a concept, the only way one knows whether *go*, *going*, *goes*, *gone* or *went* is intended is through context or finger spelling.

Many educators prefer using finger spelling with lipreading in order to develop the child's English. By using finger spelling, the emphasis is upon words and their arrangement, not just concepts.

Learning to finger spell is for some people more difficult than learning signs. Certainly reading finger spelling is far more difficult than reading signs. Nevertheless, if the student approaches the task with the proper attitude, his job will be infinitely easier.

The beginner usually makes the mistake of equating speed with fluency. Speed is not the primary goal. Just as in typewriting, our goal is rhythm, and accuracy, not speed. As one learns to finger spell accurately and rhythmically, his speed will increase naturally. Therefore, the first axiom is: Do not rush, set a rhythmic pace comfortable for yourself and stick to it.

Another common error the beginner usually commits might be facetiously called starched fingers. Many people seem to lapse into a state of shock and their fingers appear stiff as sticks. In spite of all their efforts, they just are not able to get their fingers to cooperate. For this there is only one cure—relaxation. How one manages to relax is extremely personal.

As one practices, he gains confidence in himself and becomes more relaxed. If he consciously strives to relax his stiff fingers, he can usually do so. A great deal of the stiffness stems from the premature urge to hurry. Keep this urge under control and relaxation will come.

Reading finger spelling is, for the beginner, the most difficult part of manual communication. At first, what he sees is a string of letters with no breaks in them to indicate groupings. He just cannot see where one word leaves off and another begins. He sees only individual letters, not words. Practice and time are the only cures for this.

A deaf person skilled in manual communication rarely sees individual letters. He discerns the minute pauses between words and sees words as groupings of letters. I have heard beginning finger spellers remark over and over, that just when they feel they will never be able to read finger spelling, they suddenly break through the fog, and from then on they see words, not individual letters.

I do not understand this phenomenon, though I have seen it occur many times. They go to bed one evening seeing individual letters and awaken in the morning seeing groups of letters—words. This does not happen in all cases. Furthermore, it happens only after long, arduous days of constant practice and effort. There is, therefore, no point in sitting around waiting for this benediction. It is the reward of hard work.

The object, of course, is to reach the point where one does see groups of letters much in the same way as we do when we read writing. At first, one may see only the beginning of a word, "n-e-i . . . ," and perhaps the end, ". . . o-r." From the context of the sentence "My nei . . . or makes telephone calls for me," we fill in the gap and come up with *neighbor*.

There is no short cut. Only through intensive practice will the student reach the place where he is reading words, not letters.

Other Aspects of Manual Communication

We have all experienced the deadening boredom of listening to a speaker who speaks in a monotonous voice with sparse inflection. This happens in manual communication. Just as there are colorless vocal speakers, there are colorless manual speakers. The ability to mix into signs and finger spelling other aspects which add color and life—and thus more meaning—is truly the distinguishing hall mark of a good manual communicator.

As deaf people communicate, their attention is focused on the face. They do not look at the hands, as the beginning student usually does. The face is the focal point. Therefore, it carries most of the burden of enriching the meaning of signs and finger spelling. The student must train his face to be so pliable that with wrinkles, eyebrows, eyes and mouth he can display a multitude of meanings. It must become automatic for him to sign "bad" and at the same instant have a deep furrowed frown on his face, or if the meaning dictates, a raised, questioning eyebrow.

Our voices rise and fall to add meaning to our words. The face functions for manual communication as the inflections of the voice for words. Imagine how much meaning would be lost if we did not have these inflections. The face must make these inflections visible to the eye. Facial expressions are not just amusing and entertaining, they are vital. The student must learn to ask or answer a question with his face as well as his hands.

There are other parts of the body that play important roles, especially the shoulders. Hundreds of ideas are suggested, even among hearing people, by the merest shrug of the shoulders. Mainly strive to keep them relaxed and ready to accentuate your arm movements and complement the facial expressions.

Strange as it seems, the legs also play important roles. The bending of the knees, the hunching of the shoulders, the strained facial expression on the bowed head can turn the sign "sick" into "desperately ill." One's knees are valuable adjuncts in adding depth to a sign.

Even the lowly feet must be ever alert to add their emphasis. Standing one foot on tiptoe, knees bent, etc. can change the sign for "perfect" into "precisely" or "exact." Shifting the feet often makes clear the persons speaking in a dialogue. It should be added that stamping a foot is a common way of getting a deaf person's attention.

The hands and arms of course play the leading role. They express the noun, as it were, and the other parts of the body supply the modifying aspects. The vigor with which a sign is made may express anger or docility, fear or joy. The speed with which the sign is made may convey the feeling of great haste, or fear, or peace, or laziness.

The modifying aspects are perhaps the most difficult to learn. Many people cannot overcome their lifelong inhibitions to express their emotions thus in public. They may still communicate very well with deaf people in spite of this. Nevertheless, the ability to add these modifiers makes the communication easier and more pleasurable and adds much more depth to meaning. One should do as much of it as one can.

A final note here to prevent misunderstanding. The modifying aspects do not actually change the meaning of the signs. The concept represented by the sign remains the same. Remember that a deaf person does not think the word *sick* when he sees the sign "sick," he gets immediate meaning from the sign without the intermediate need for translation. So naturally, "sick," does not actually become "desperately ill" when modified as described previously. What happens is that fine nuances are added to deepen or intensify the meaning of the sign. The deaf person understands that the person did not just have a stomach ache, but was really bad off.

These modifying aspects cannot be taught in a book. They must be learned by observation, imitation and practice until one catches the feel of it, the spirit. Then they become so automatic that one is unaware that one is doing them.

The Plan of the Lessons

Although different teachers at different times and places have made efforts to standardize the sign language, no widespread concerted standardization program has been undertaken. Because of this, some signs used in one locality might not be used in another locality. There are, however, not so many of these signs as to make comprehension difficult. The student must learn the sign that is used in his own locality, whenever there is a contradiction.

In these lessons, you are sometimes given a choice of several ways of making a sign. No attempt is made in these lessons to standardize signs. The choice of how to make a sign was based entirely on what the author believes to be those most commonly used among deaf people. He claims no infallibility.

Dr. William C. Stokoe, chairman of the English Department of Gallaudet College, points out in his book, *Sign Language Structure*, that most signs have three parts: (1) the shape of the hands, (2) the place where the hands move to and from and (3) the movements. This observation has been utilized in planning the lessons in this manual. Beginning with lesson six, most of the lessons are built around only one handshape. That is, all the signs in the lesson have the same handshape. Only the movements and places will change from one sign to another. By keeping one part of the sign constant and varying the other two parts, it is believed that the student will learn the signs more quickly and remember than more easily.

In the practice sentences, certain words are underlined. This means that you have been taught the sign for that word. You are, therefore, to be held responsible for knowing it. Always sign the underlined words, fingerspell those that are not underlined. Sometimes two words are underlined together. This means that there is one sign which conveys the meaning for both words.

Sometimes more than one word is given for a sign. If the words are separated by a comma (,) this means that the words are synonyms. If the words are separated by a semi-colon (;), this means that the sign has more than one meaning. Each word set off by a semi-colon is a different meaning for the sign. *Please note* that no attempt has been made to list all the synonyms or all the different meanings for each sign. We do attempt to do this in the *Index*, but we do not claim this index to be all encompassing.

A Note to the Teacher (which we strongly advise all students to read).

Practice material is provided in each lesson. Once a lesson has been covered, and the student has practiced it as his homework assignment, hold the student responsible for mastery of the practice material. There is little point in covering new material before "old" material is mastered. If the student is serious about learning manual communication, he must be willing to practice the material on his own time until he masters it.

Some pictures show the hands as they are viewed by the signer. Other pictures give the view of the receiver, or of a third party.

LESSON 1
The American Manual Alphabet
(As seen by the finger speller)

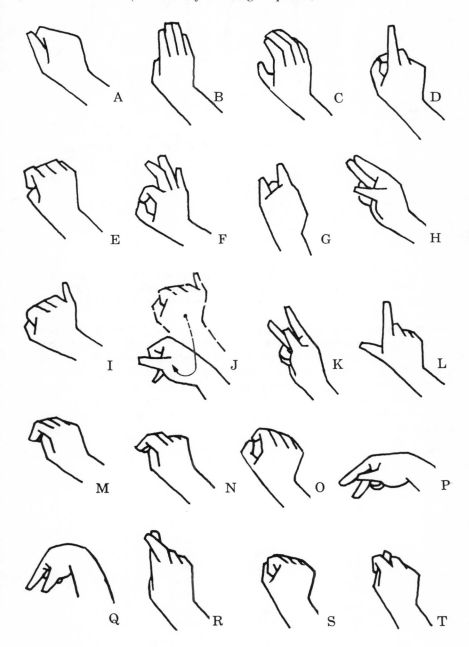

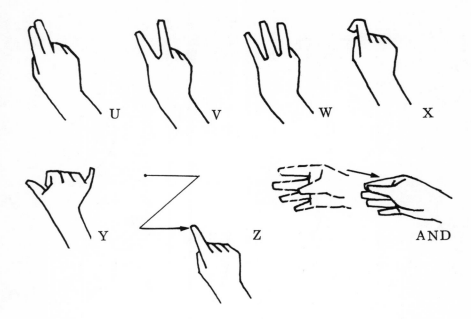

U V W X

Y Z AND

1. The goals in mastering the alphabet are accuracy and smoothness in making the letters. *Do not be concerned with speed.* Strive for a *rhythm* in making the letters and speed will come naturally in good time.

There should be a smooth transition from one letter to the next with no pausing between. It is at this point that rhythm plays a vital part. Pick a uniform, constant rhythm that is not too fast or too slow for you. Then, stick to that rhythmical pattern. Force yourself to do this. You may have to go slowly at first, but that is preferable to a fast-slow-and-complete stop pattern. It is confusing to read a person who spells alternately fast and slow within a single word. Travel at a constant speed.

Practice words

boy	beg	lap
jig	fed	man
box	ate	nut
adz	had	one
for	cut	pen
ear	did	sun
him	gar	try
hue	ink	view
rag	kid	want

2. Letters to be particularly careful about are *g*, *k* and *p*. There are two accepted ways to make a *g*. There are two accepted ways of making *p*. Confusion sometimes arises when distinguishing between *k* and one of the forms for *p*.

keep-package	pick-help
fig-back	people-kipper
pig-page	laugh-poker

3. The end of a word is denoted by holding the last letter in the word about one extra beat of your rhythmical pattern, then proceeding immediately to the first letter of the next word. It is unnecessary and confusing to drop the hand after each word.

4. When double letters occur within the word, there are several ways to treat them, depending upon the formation of the fingers.

A. With z make the movement twice.

   fuzzy   buzz   fizz   Ozzie   dazzle   embezzle

B. When formations require the thumb and a finger to touch each other, or require a closed fist, then open or relax the fingers and repeat the formation.

Spell these words:

Aaron	gee
been	loose
off	gutter
fuss	Eddy
Baal	effort
seen	boss
booze	battery
kettle	ruddy
Paar	afford
deem	crass
look	Hoffman
mitten	biddy
Padden	cuff
feel	sissy
tool	toddy
bottle	stiff
Ladder	essay

C. Other formations are doubled by simply moving the hand slightly to the right in a "bumpy" fashion.

5. When a word ends with the same letter which begins the next word, it is shown by slightly opening the hand and then remaking the letter, or by just slightly relaxing the hand and always moving the hand slightly to the side.

keep - pill	to - other
ever - run	been - napping
still - life	tea - at
happy - year	kick - Karl
tunic - can	bed - down
see - Earl	stiff - foil
base - seem	not - tired
Tim - might	cough - hard
saw - what	jazz - zoo

Practice Sentences

Pack my box with five dozen jugs of liquid veneer.
Jack Powers was quite vexed by their lazy farming.
Jim quietly picked six zippers from the woven bag.
The six jets took off with a wail of engines and, like queenly comets, zoomed up far above us.
It is rumored that five or six squadrons from this wing will sortie to La Paz and back in July.
The plane crews quickly move from the flight deck just before the sizzling fuses will explode.

Note to the Student (which the teachers might also read).

It is *extremely* important that the student spend a certain amount of time *daily* on the practice material provided in these lessons. The amount of time one should spend is an individual matter, but it should be enough so that the student can recite the practice material smoothly and rhymically. Neglect of sufficient practice ends in frustration at trying to learn new signs before old signs are mastered.

This admonishment is so important, we feel the need to emphasize it by repeating it.

4

LESSON 2

Numbers
(As seen by persons other than the person making them)

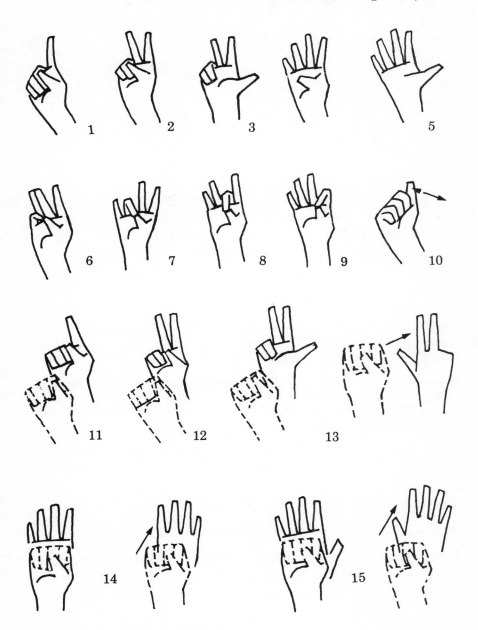

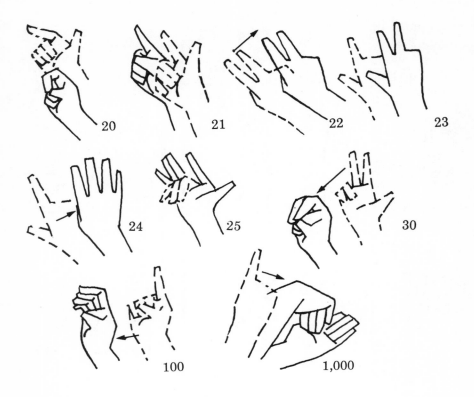

The formation of the numbers may be made with the palm facing the signer or the receiver. There is no fixed principle. Often 1-5 are done with the palm toward the signer.

Numbers 11 and 12 are usually made with the palm in. Numbers 13-19 begin with the palm in, but end with the palm out.
It can be seen that the "teens" are a combination of the formation for "10" plus the number.

The twenties are perhaps the most difficult decade to do. The thumb and index finger constitute the "2" in "20" rather than the index and middle finger.

The rest of the decades are done normally.

Approximation of numbers are shown by shaking the number.

Hundreds are noted by the letter "C." One hundred would be signed "1C," two hundred "2C," and so on. Millions and billions are repetitions of the thousand sign.

Anything above the billion sign should be spelled if accuracy is desired. To indicate an exaggerated number far beyond the billions, repeat the thousand sign a sufficient number of times until the desired impression has been conveyed.

Years are signed just as they are spoken: 1961—"nineteen sixty-one."

1961

Practice

57	Do these as years, not as numbers
83	
99	1918
100	1961
651	1874
321	1776
2,001	2010
8,564	1660
9,214	1492
1,000,230	1506
3,687,391	1920
"thirties"	1819
"around 50"	1321

LESSON 3

NOTE: Before getting into formal lessons, which begin with Lesson 6, it is helpful to learn to sign the pronouns, some prepositions and conjunctions and some ways of negating statements. These will be covered in this and the next two lessons.

HE, SHE, IT (fingerspell)

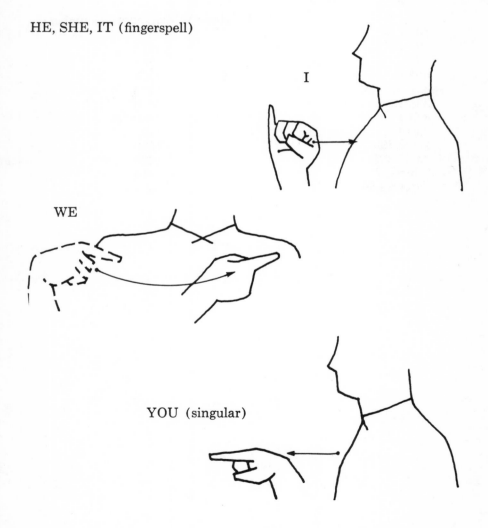

I

WE

YOU (singular)

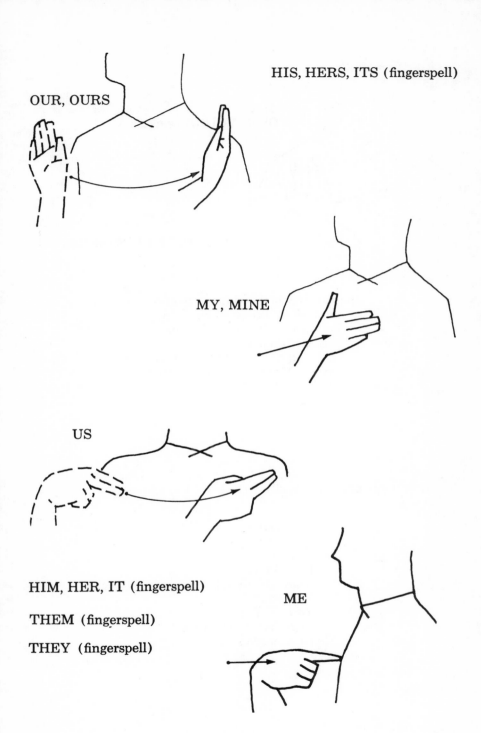

OUR, OURS

HIS, HERS, ITS (fingerspell)

MY, MINE

US

HIM, HER, IT (fingerspell)

THEM (fingerspell)

THEY (fingerspell)

ME

9

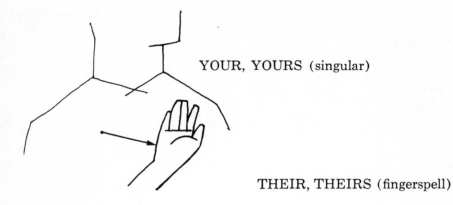

YOUR, YOURS (singular)

THEIR, THEIRS (fingerspell)

NOTE: When the third person or persons or things about which you are talking are actually present, then you may use the same signs that are used for "you." Make the sign towards the third person or thing.

Practice: (sign and fingerspell)

You and I.
We see you.
Did he see it?
He told you?
They are theirs.
Is it yours?
You must try.
Together we shall go.
Do you see them?

LESSON 4

CONNECTIVES

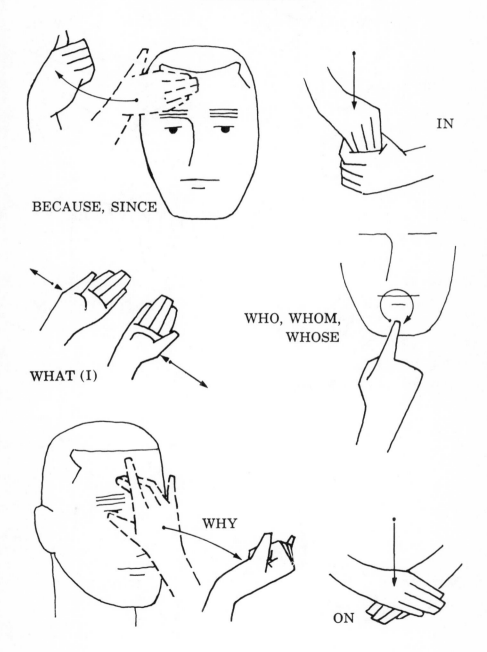

BECAUSE, SINCE

IN

WHAT (I)

WHO, WHOM, WHOSE

WHY

ON

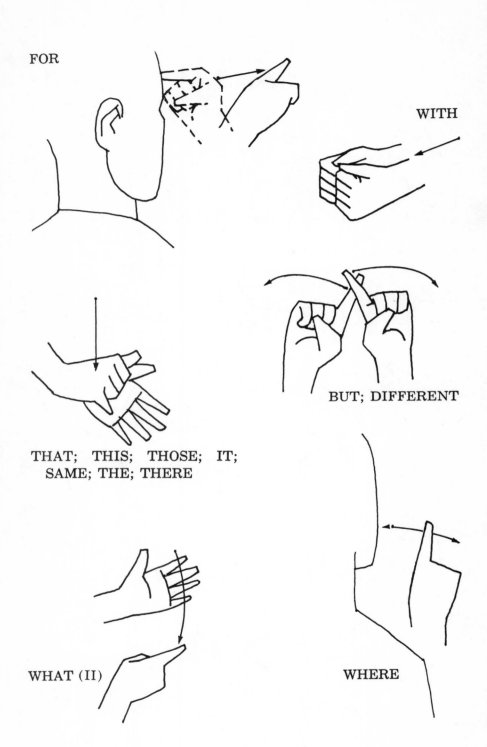

FOR

WITH

BUT; DIFFERENT

THAT; THIS; THOSE; IT;
SAME; THE; THERE

WHAT (II)

WHERE

12

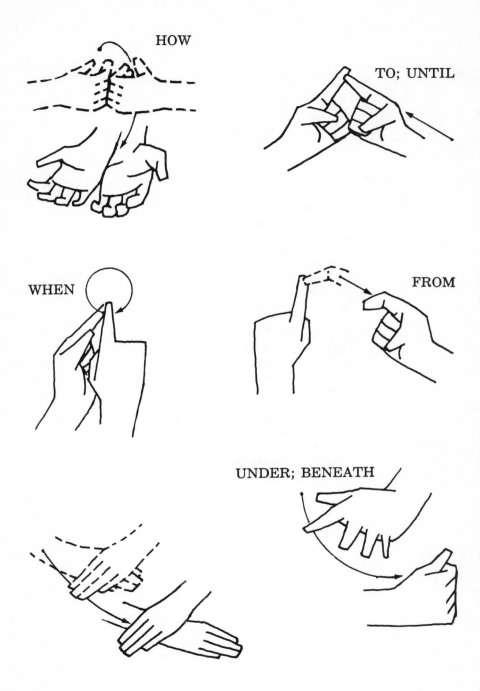

HOW

TO; UNTIL

WHEN

FROM

UNDER; BENEATH

INTO, IN

13

Practice:

How are you?
How old are you?
Give it to him.
Why did they go?
Here comes that man.
Give me that book.
The man came with me.
Take off your hat.
What is your name?
When is your birthday?
That's what I told him.
He is from Texas.
Because he was sick.
That's not true.
He is at the movies.
I have been here since four.
   (NOTE: "since" in this sen-
   tence does not mean "be-
   cause," so do not sign it,
   fingerspell it.)

LESSON 5
NEGATIVES

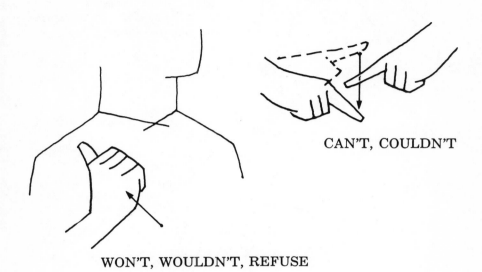

CAN'T, COULDN'T

WON'T, WOULDN'T, REFUSE

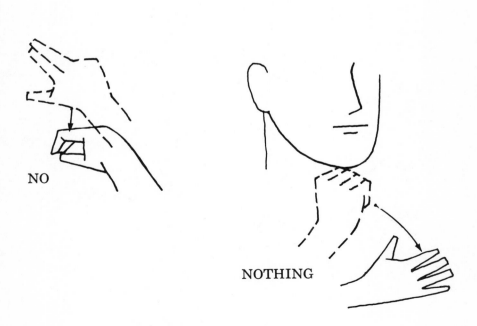

NO

NOTHING

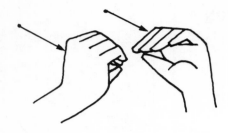

NONE, NO (To answer the question, "How many?" "How much?" use this sign to express the idea of "not any.")

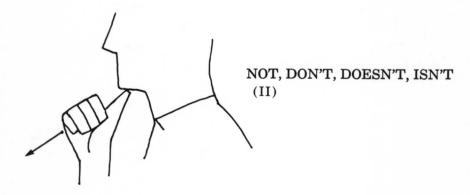

NOT, DON'T, DOESN'T, ISN'T
(I)

NOT, DON'T, DOESN'T, ISN'T
(II)

Practice:

I won't go, because you are
going.
Who cannot stay until we are
finished?
She doesn't know where he is.
Why did no one come with
you? (Note: Here "no one"
is to be signed "none.")
No, I don't see how I can.
There is nothing good on TV.
No, you can't go.
That isn't what I said.

LESSON 6

ACROSS; AFTER

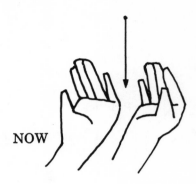

NOW

CLEAN; NICE

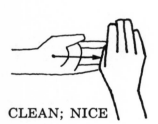

COLLEGE

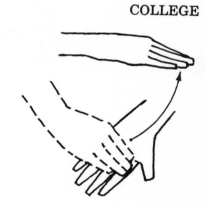

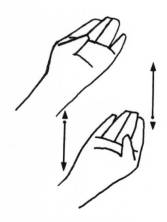

PERHAPS, MAYBE

BRING

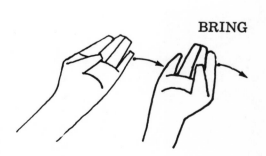

18

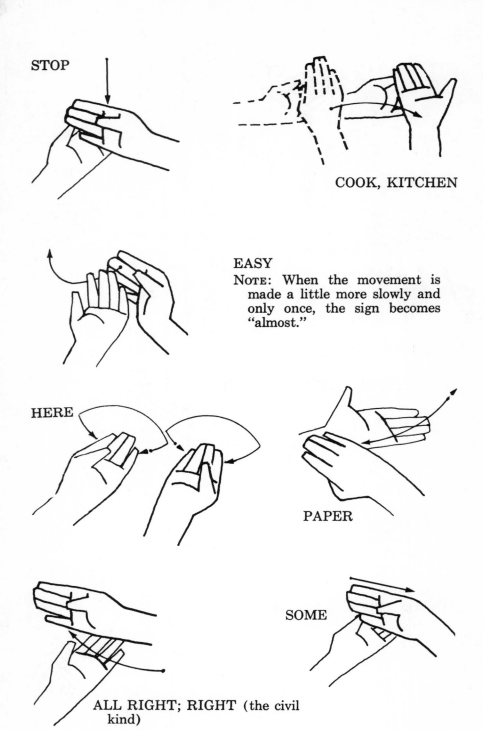

STOP

COOK, KITCHEN

EASY
NOTE: When the movement is made a little more slowly and only once, the sign becomes "almost."

HERE

PAPER

ALL RIGHT; RIGHT (the civil kind)

SOME

BUY

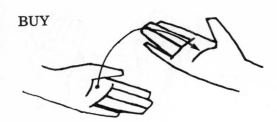

THROUGH

MONEY

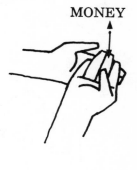

LESSON, CHAPTER, COURSE

PARDON, EXCUSE, FORGIVE

SCHOOL

Practice:

Excuse me, but where is the snackbar?

Did you clean your room?

Do you have a clean piece of paper?

Where is your school?

How do you like college?

Stop fingerspelling so fast!

That's all right with me.

I can't cross the road.

I want some too.

I go through this every year.

What courses will you take?

It costs a lot of money to go to college.

You will need money to buy clothes.

College is not as easy as school.

Maybe you will not finish college.

Now you know that is all right.

I doubt that you can buy a car here.

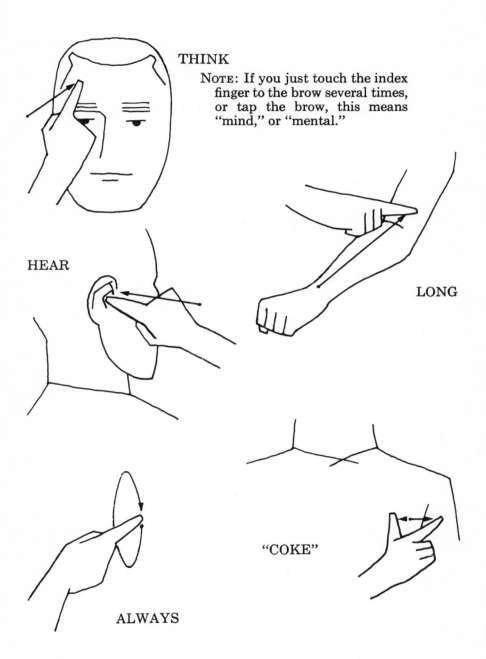

THINK

NOTE: If you just touch the index finger to the brow several times, or tap the brow, this means "mind," or "mental."

HEAR

LONG

"COKE"

ALWAYS

22

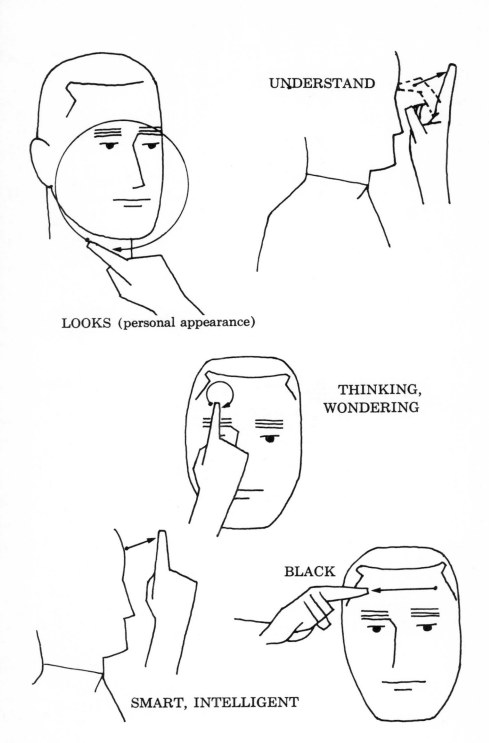

UNDERSTAND

LOOKS (personal appearance)

THINKING, WONDERING

BLACK

SMART, INTELLIGENT

Practice:

I wonder why he said that?
I thought we were going to the
   movies.
I can't understand him.
My brother is very smart.
Our cat is black as coal.
I heard that he is leaving.
There are 24 "Cokes" in one
   case.
From what I hear, it is always
   hot here.
Who said I look sick?
I think black looks good on
   you.

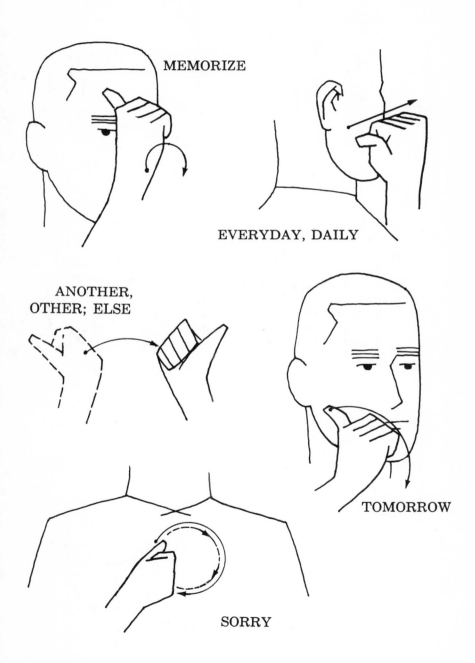

MEMORIZE

EVERYDAY, DAILY

ANOTHER,
OTHER; ELSE

TOMORROW

SORRY

YESTERDAY

ANY

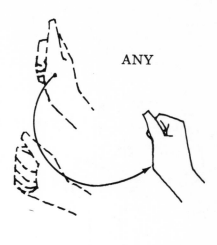

HANDKERCHIEF; COLD
(virus type)

NOTE: When the movement in-
cludes the nod of the head and
the right hand continues holding the nose, it means to be
"fooled," or "tricked."

CANADA

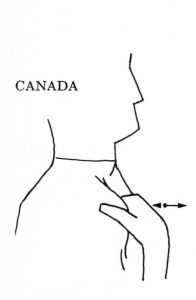

SECRET

PRIDE

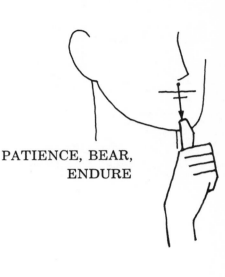

PATIENCE, BEAR,
ENDURE

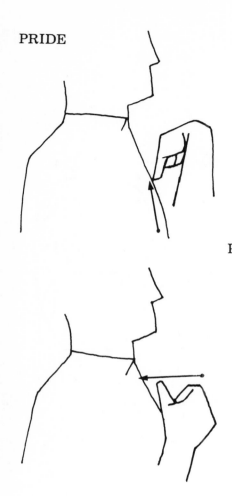

MYSELF

NOTE: "Yourself" may be done by pushing the *10* handshape toward the person to whom you are speaking. You may also express "itself," "himself," "themselves," etc. in this way.

Practice:

You better memorize your lesson.
All right, I will be in class everyday.
Tomorrow I will buy a pair of pants.
It was hot yesterday.
Do you have a cold?

Be patient, tomorrow will come.
It is easy to say, "I am sorry."
Are you from Canada?
I will do it myself.
Study so that your parents will be proud of you.
What else can I do?

DURING, WHILE

BROTHER

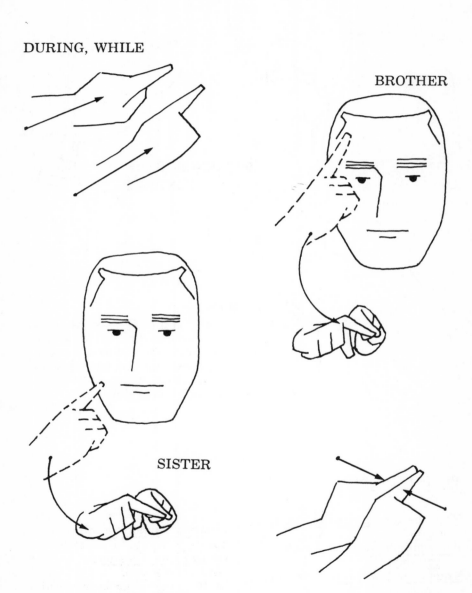

SISTER

ALIKE, LIKE, SAME, AS

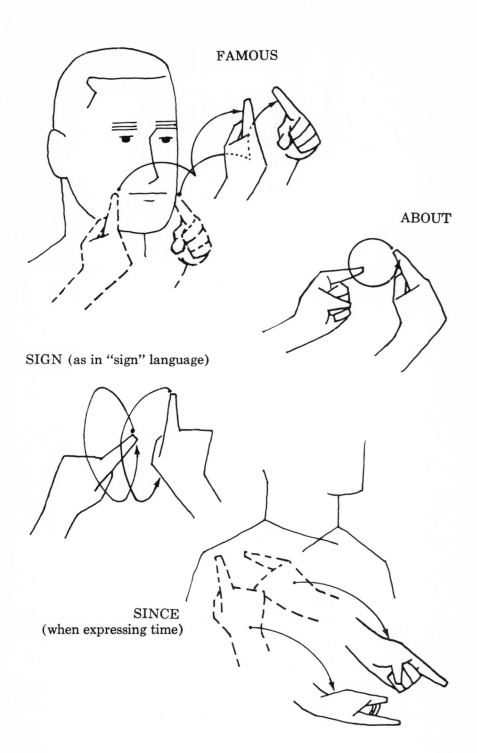

FAMOUS

ABOUT

SIGN (as in "sign" language)

SINCE
(when expressing time)

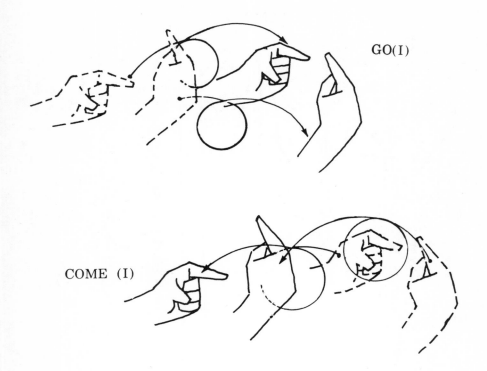

GO(I)

COME (I)

Practice:

You go with him while I stay
  here.
He looks as if he is ill.
Did you see one like it?
He looks like his brother.
Your sister is pretty.
Can you sign very well?
Why won't you come?
If you don't come, I won't go.
There were about 39 boys and
  13 girls here.
When you are famous, you may
  do what you like.
My brother has refused to talk
  to my sister since 1950.

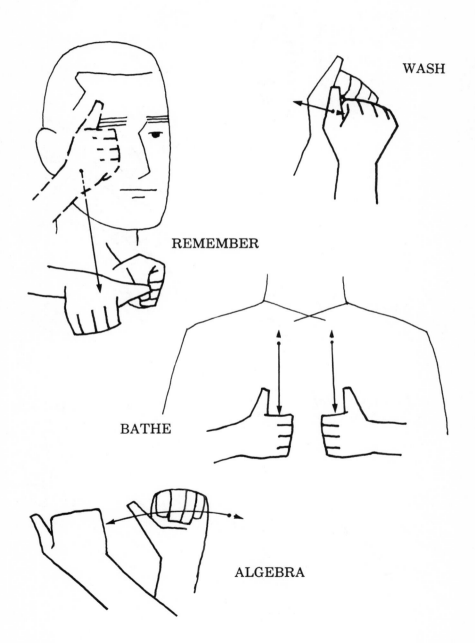

WASH

REMEMBER

BATHE

ALGEBRA

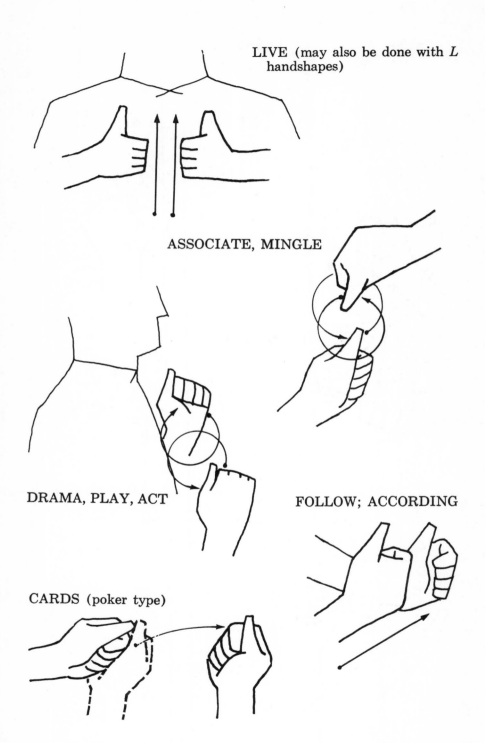

LIVE (may also be done with *L* handshapes)

ASSOCIATE, MINGLE

DRAMA, PLAY, ACT

FOLLOW; ACCORDING

CARDS (poker type)

32

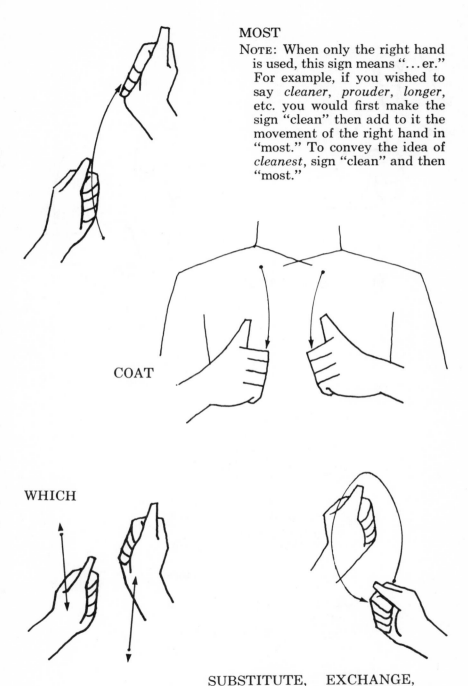

MOST

NOTE: When only the right hand is used, this sign means "...er." For example, if you wished to say *cleaner*, *prouder*, *longer*, etc. you would first make the sign "clean" then add to it the movement of the right hand in "most." To convey the idea of *cleanest*, sign "clean" and then "most."

COAT

WHICH

SUBSTITUTE, EXCHANGE, TRADE

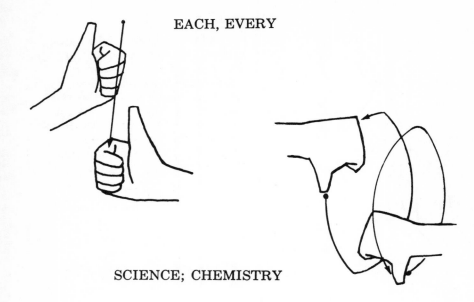

EACH, EVERY

SCIENCE; CHEMISTRY

Practice:

Did you see the play?
I almost forgot my coat.
Does everyone know me?
Why are you following me?
Which dress will you buy?
He took most of it with him.
I play cards almost every night.
Don't be afraid to mingle with
    other deaf people.
You will take a course in chem-
    istry.
I bought a new pair of shoes
    yesterday.
Some people don't understand
    algebra.
Where can I wash my clothes?
Do you remember the lesson
    from yesterday?
Life is not always easy.
Did you take a bath yesterday?

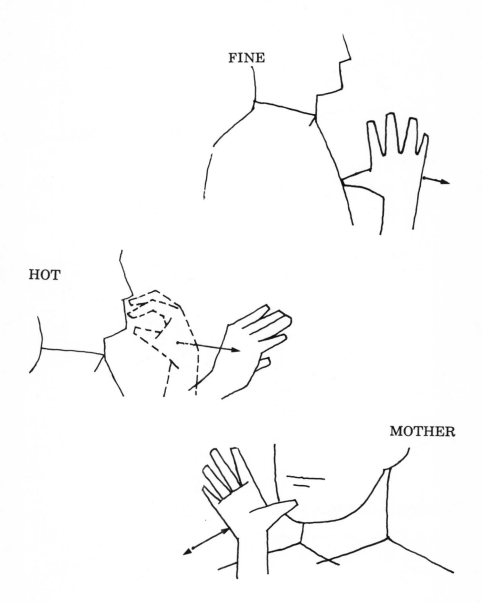

FINE

HOT

MOTHER

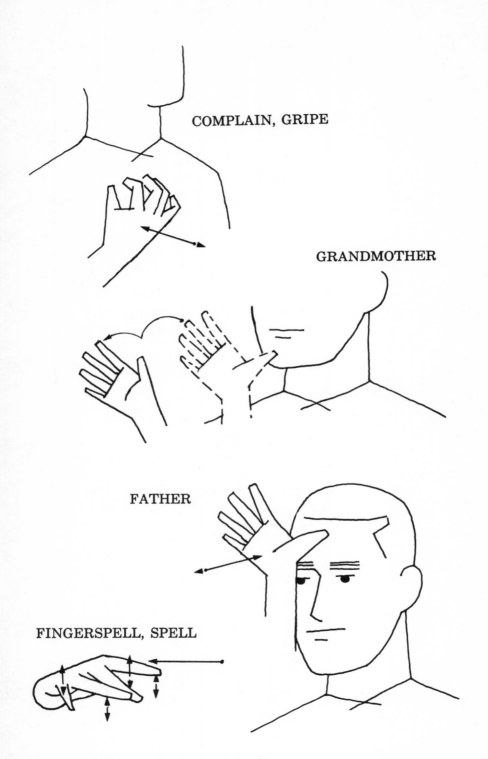

COMPLAIN, GRIPE

GRANDMOTHER

FATHER

FINGERSPELL, SPELL

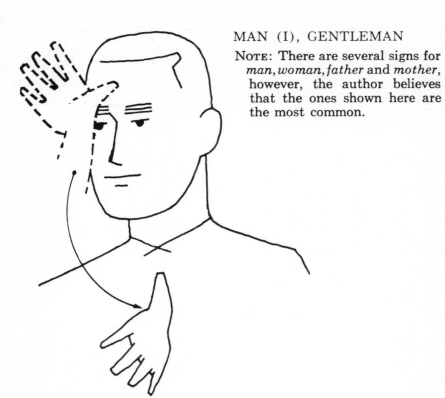

MAN (I), GENTLEMAN

NOTE: There are several signs for *man, woman, father* and *mother*, however, the author believes that the ones shown here are the most common.

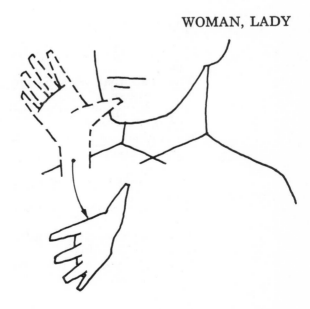

WOMAN, LADY

GRANDFATHER

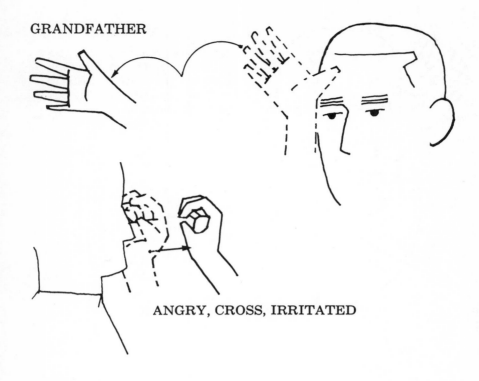

ANGRY, CROSS, IRRITATED

Practice:

Who was that man?
That man is my father.
My grandfather came from Ire-
land.
Why does that woman come
here everyday?
What did your mother say
when she came?
My brother and I will visit our
grandmother.
You look fine.
I can't understand fingerspell-
ing.
I dread summer because it is so
hot.
What are you so cross about?
He always looks angry.
Why gripe, you can't do any-
thing about it.

SHOES

HABIT

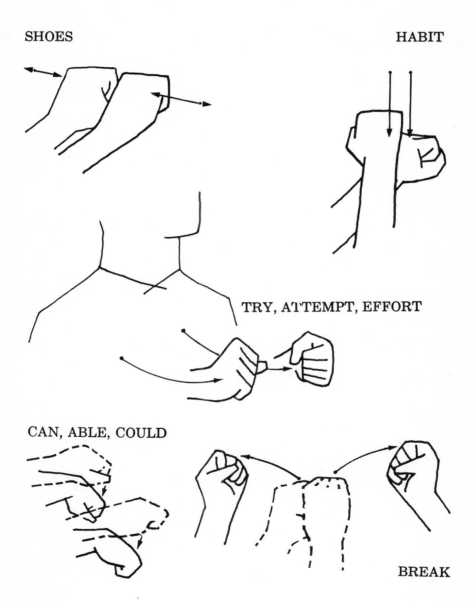

TRY, ATTEMPT, EFFORT

CAN, ABLE, COULD

BREAK

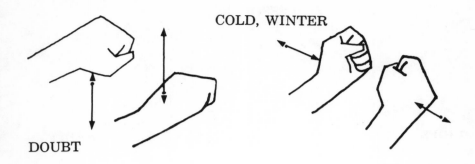

COLD, WINTER

DOUBT

EXERCISE

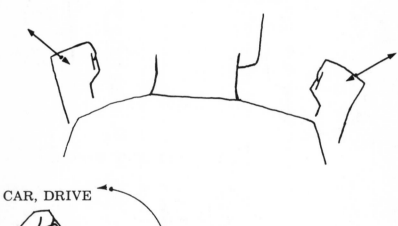

CAR, DRIVE

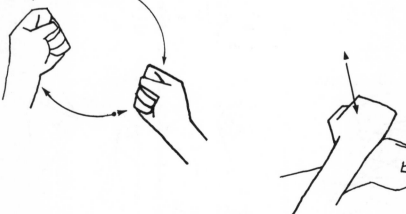

WORK, JOB

Practice:

Try to win everyday.
Can you play with us tomor-
row?
February is a very cold month.
What kind of car does your
friend have?
Boys and girls need exercise
everyday.
Try to form good habits in col-
lege.
What kind of work does your
friend do?
You must try to break bad
habits.
I doubt that I can do that job.
Where are my black shoes?

SAD

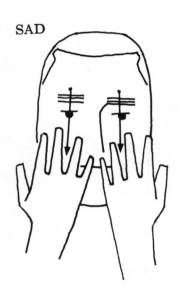

FIRE, BURN

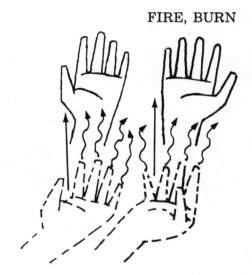

BASKETBALL

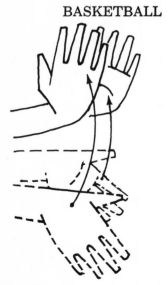

AMERICA

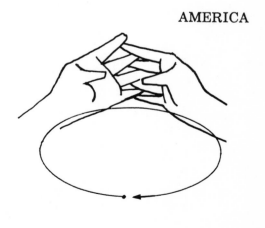

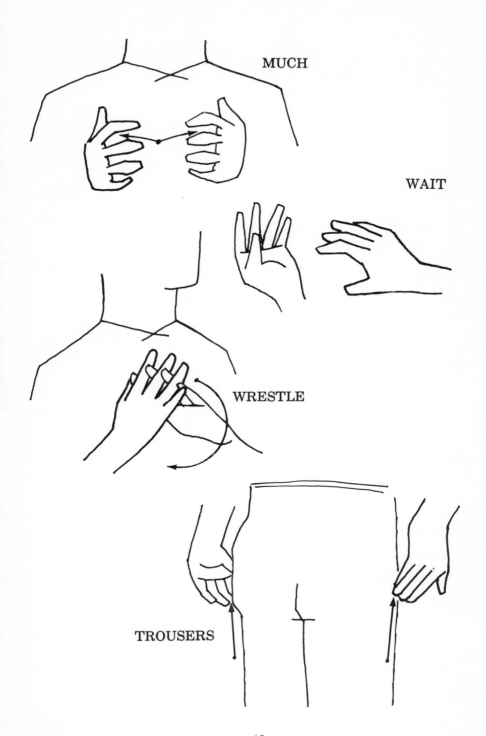

MUCH

WAIT

WRESTLE

TROUSERS

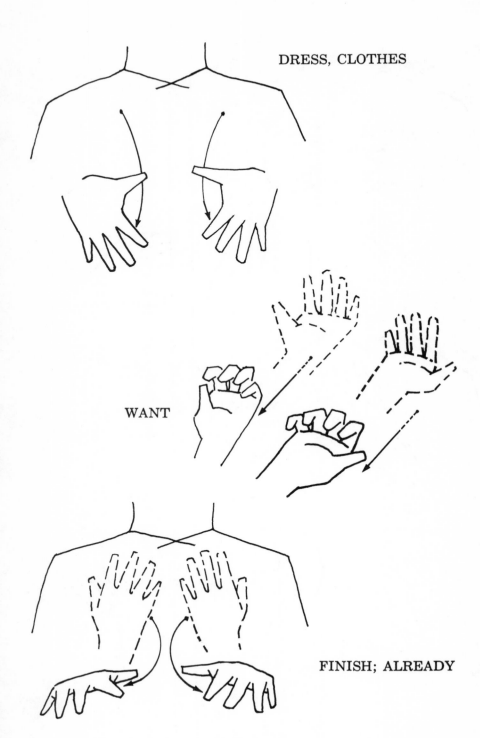

DRESS, CLOTHES

WANT

FINISH; ALREADY

44

LEAVE

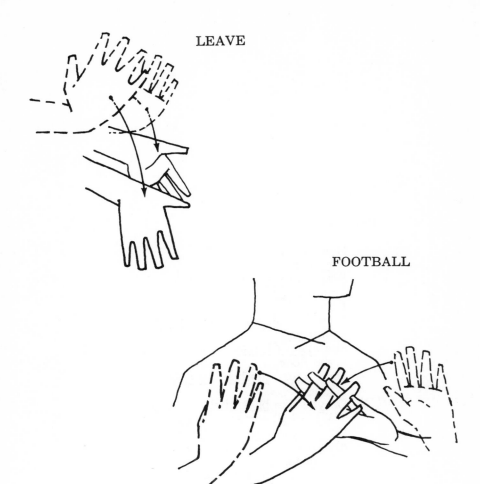

FOOTBALL

FRIGHTEN, SCARE, AFRAID

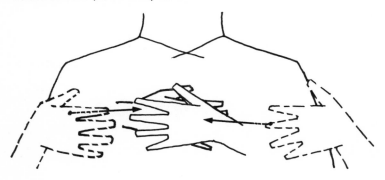

45

Practice:

How did the fire start?
Why is he sad?
What are you waiting for?
I want a Coke.
I finished my work.
I have already met your
  brother.
She always leaves her coat on
  the floor.
Did your mother complain
  much?
Do you like basketball?
The football game was long.
Do you know how to wrestle?
America believes in freedom
  from fear.
Are you through dressing?
You didn't scare me much.
Your pants are dirty.

LESSON 14

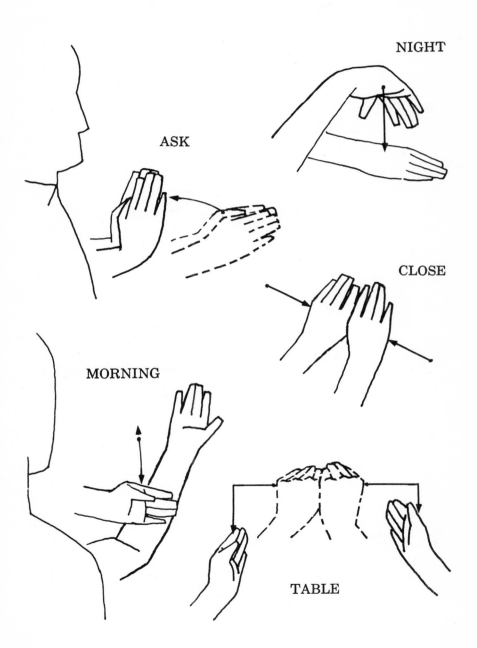

NIGHT

ASK

CLOSE

MORNING

TABLE

47

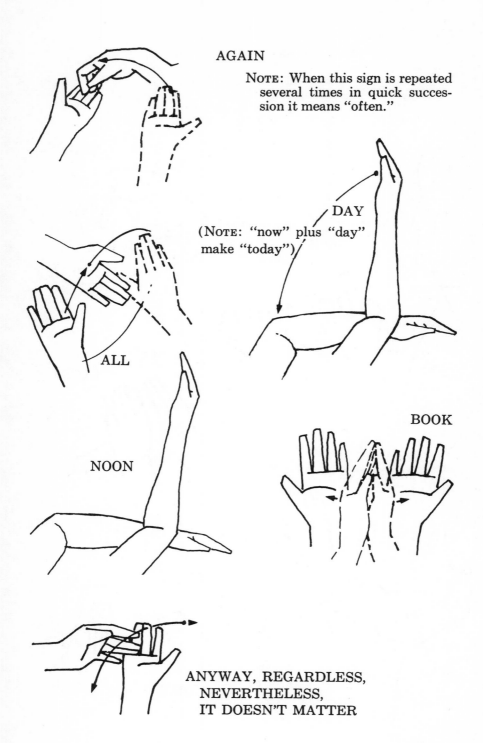

AGAIN

NOTE: When this sign is repeated several times in quick succession it means "often."

DAY

(NOTE: "now" plus "day" make "today")

ALL

NOON

BOOK

ANYWAY, REGARDLESS,
NEVERTHELESS,
IT DOESN'T MATTER

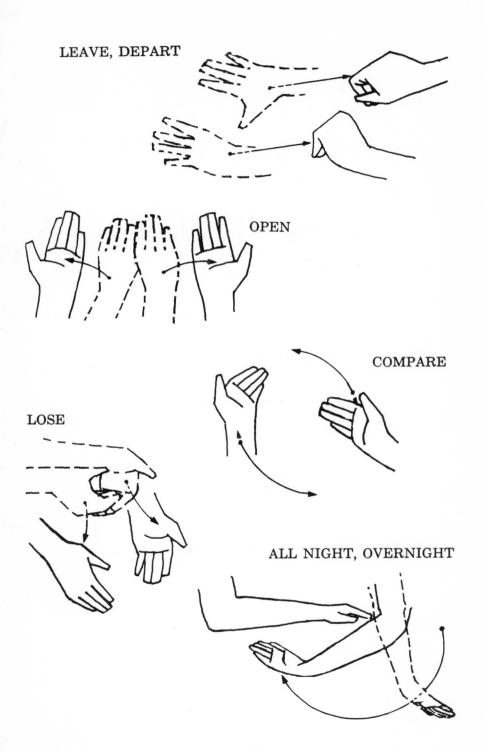

LEAVE, DEPART

OPEN

COMPARE

LOSE

ALL NIGHT, OVERNIGHT

Practice:

Did you buy the book?

Don't compare the past with the future.

Will you open the box?

Please close the door easily. (NOTE: "close the door" is done with one sign.)

Don't put your shoes on the table.

Don't leave until you are ready.

Pardon me, did you lose your coat?

You must all work hard.

I can't see through that window.

What day did you catch a cold?

Good morning.

We will meet the girls tomorrow afternoon.

Have you eaten today?

Good night.

We worked on our chemistry all night.

I am going, no matter what you think.

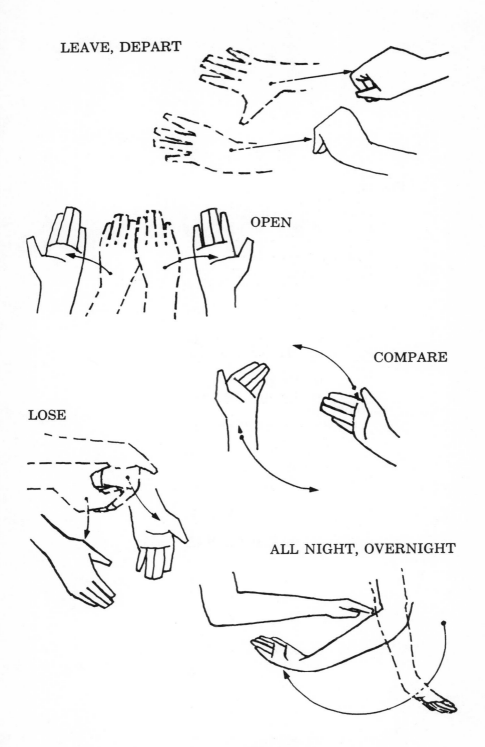

LEAVE, DEPART

OPEN

COMPARE

LOSE

ALL NIGHT, OVERNIGHT

49

Practice:

Did you buy the book?
Don't compare the past with
the future.
Will you open the box?
Please close the door easily.
(NOTE: "close the door" is
done with one sign.)
Don't put your shoes on the
table.
Don't leave until you are ready.
Pardon me, did you lose your
coat?
You must all work hard.
I can't see through that win-
dow.
What day did you catch a cold?
Good morning.
We will meet the girls tomor-
row afternoon.
Have you eaten today?
Good night.
We worked on our chemistry
all night.
I am going, no matter what you
think.

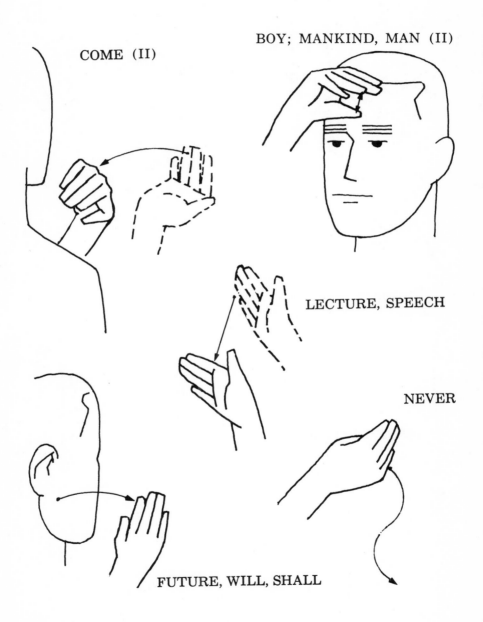

COME (II)

BOY; MANKIND, MAN (II)

LECTURE, SPEECH

NEVER

FUTURE, WILL, SHALL

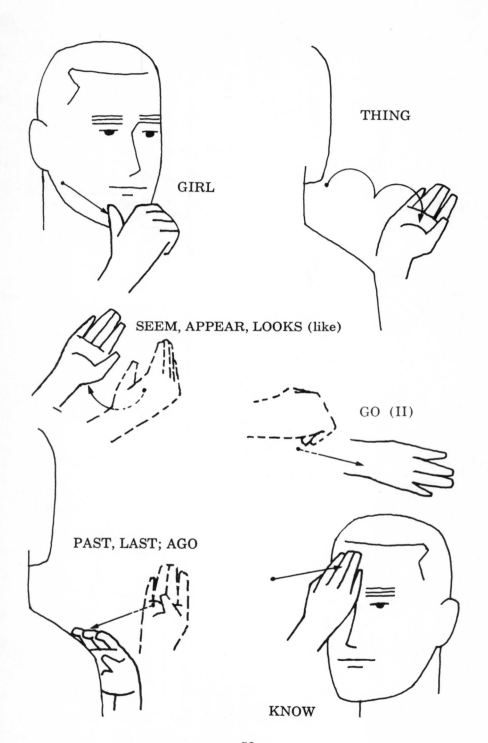

GIRL

THING

SEEM, APPEAR, LOOKS (like)

GO (II)

PAST, LAST; AGO

KNOW

52

Practice:

Where is the boy now?
Do you know how to sign?
Will you come tonight? (NOTE:
    "tonight" is "now" plus
    "night.")
That is all in the past now.
Who will lecture tonight?
Never play with fire.
We are afraid of things we
    don't understand.
It seems to me that he didn't
    finish.
Come here.
He went home yesterday.

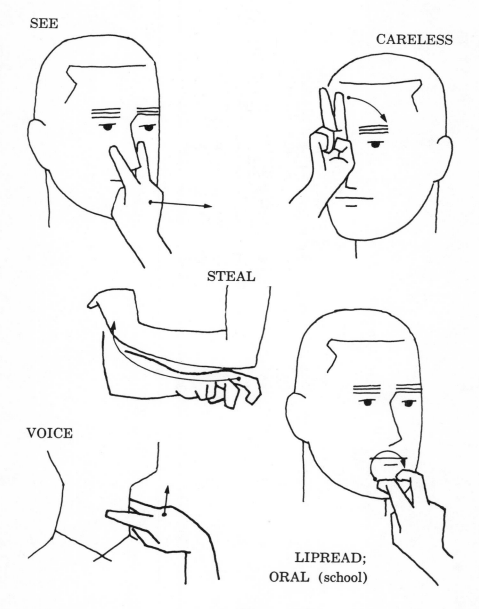

SEE

CARELESS

STEAL

VOICE

LIPREAD;
ORAL (school)

IGNORANT

MISUNDERSTAND

LOOK AT; WATCH

DISBELIEVE;
DOUBT

STUCK

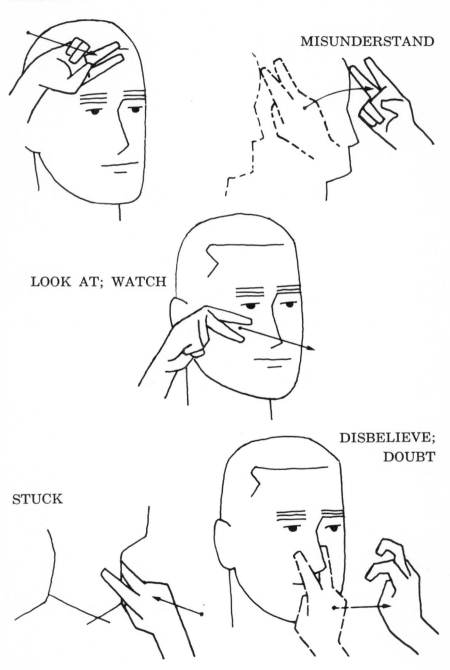

55

Practice:

Ignorance is no excuse.
Don't be careless with your
books.
Careless people often mis-
understand.
He has a bad habit of watching
too much TV.
Can you see the man?
I don't believe that book is
true.
Are you from an oral school?
He has a strong voice.
I got stuck in the mud
yesterday.
It is hard to forgive someone
who steals.

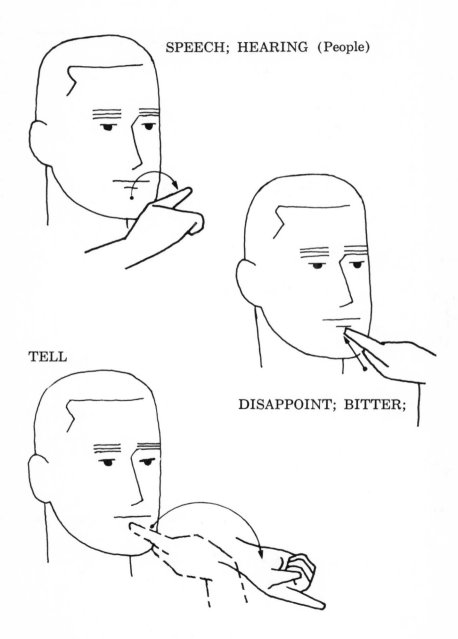

SPEECH; HEARING (People)

TELL

DISAPPOINT; BITTER;

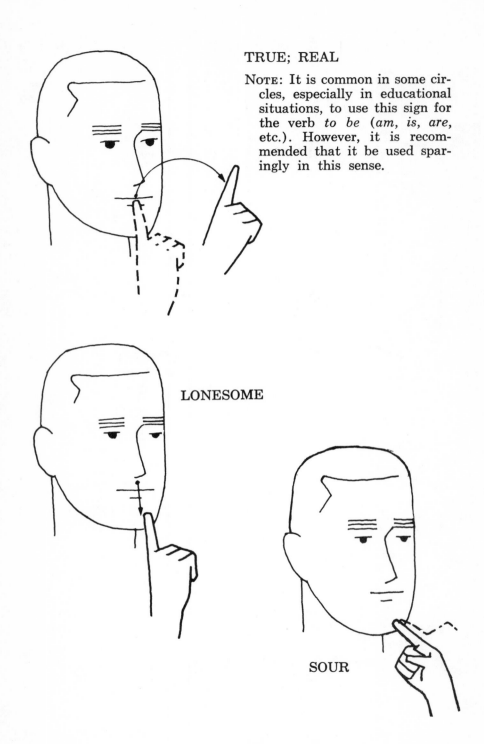

TRUE; REAL

NOTE: It is common in some circles, especially in educational situations, to use this sign for the verb *to be* (*am*, *is*, *are*, etc.). However, it is recommended that it be used sparingly in this sense.

LONESOME

SOUR

FALSE

HUSH; QUIET

RED

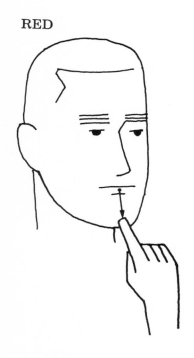

LAUGH

Practice:

> Many students get <u>lonesome</u>.
> Is it <u>true</u> <u>that</u> <u>you</u> <u>don't</u> like him?
> Be <u>quiet</u> <u>I</u> can't <u>hear</u> him.
> <u>Don't</u> make any <u>false</u> statements.
> <u>I</u> was <u>disappointed</u> because <u>I</u> <u>couldn't</u> <u>understand</u> the <u>lecture</u>.
> <u>Always</u> <u>tell</u> the <u>truth</u>.
> <u>I</u> have a <u>red</u> pen.
> <u>You</u> may <u>laugh</u>, but <u>not</u> so <u>loudly</u>.
> <u>My</u> <u>sister</u> <u>goes</u> <u>to</u> a <u>hearing</u> <u>school</u>.

ANSWER

CORRECT

NOTE: When repeated several times, it means regularly.

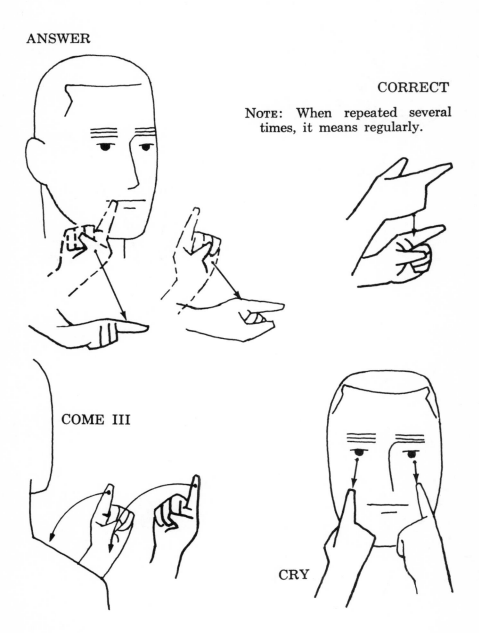

COME III

CRY

HAPPEN; ACCIDENT

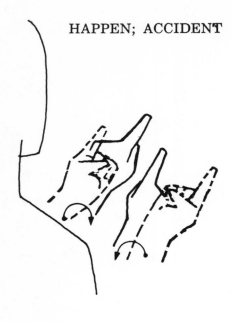

MEET (a person)

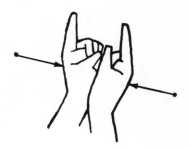

SUCCEED

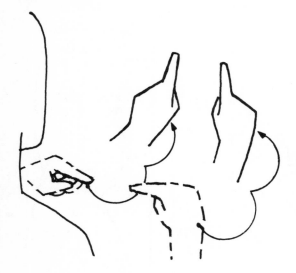

62

AGREE

TALK;
CONVERSATION;
COMMUNICATE

GO (III)

NOTE: When movement is repeated 2–3 times, it means
"attend regularly."

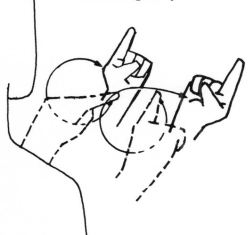

Practice:

I don't believe that is correct.
We met yesterday in school.
I tried to talk to him but I
  couldn't lipread him.
When did he come?
If you don't come, I won't go.
If at first you don't succeed,
  try, try, again.
Don't try to memorize the
  answer.
It happened in chemistry class.
I agree that all is not right.

PRETTY

EAT; FOOD

Note: "eat" + "noon" = "lunch."

SLEEP

EXPERIENCE

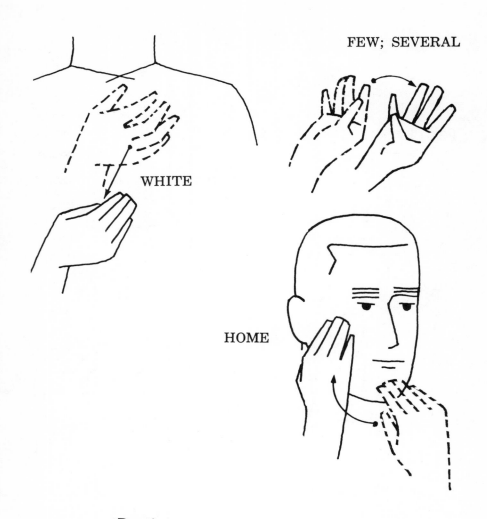

WHITE

FEW; SEVERAL

HOME

Practice:

Eat what you like.
I feel sad when I get lonesome for home.
There is no teacher like experience.
I am going to sleep early.
I never knew such a pretty girl!
In hot weather white clothing is cool.
I know a few policemen.

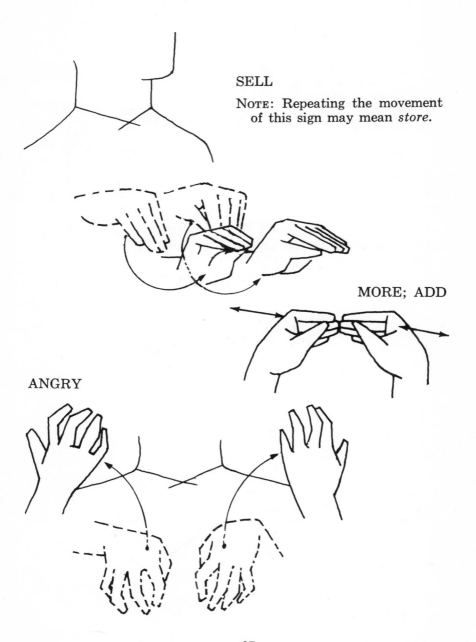

SELL

NOTE: Repeating the movement of this sign may mean *store*.

MORE; ADD

ANGRY

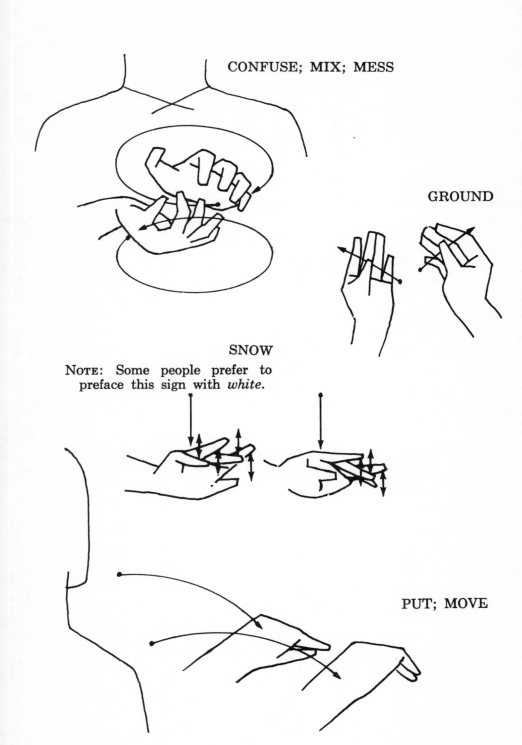

CONFUSE; MIX; MESS

GROUND

SNOW

NOTE: Some people prefer to preface this sign with *white*.

PUT; MOVE

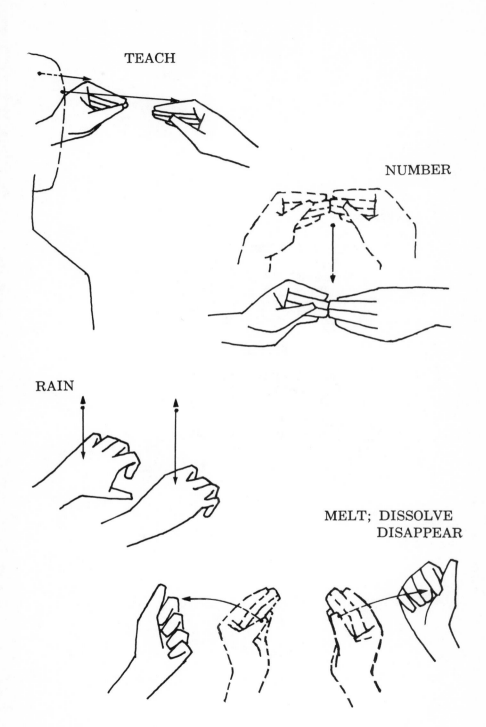

TEACH

NUMBER

RAIN

MELT; DISSOLVE
DISAPPEAR

69

Practice:

I doubt that he can teach me.
I must buy some more paper.
What number are we on now?
I sold my books yesterday.
Put your money on the table.
The ground is cold in December.
My money disappeared overnight.
I am mad because I couldn't do my algebra.
The first days in college are always confusing.
Maybe we will get more rain tomorrow.
It snowed almost 4 inches yesterday.

LESSON 21

HAPPY

PLEASE; ENJOY

SUGAR; SWEET;
CUTE; CANDY

BED

GOOD; WELL

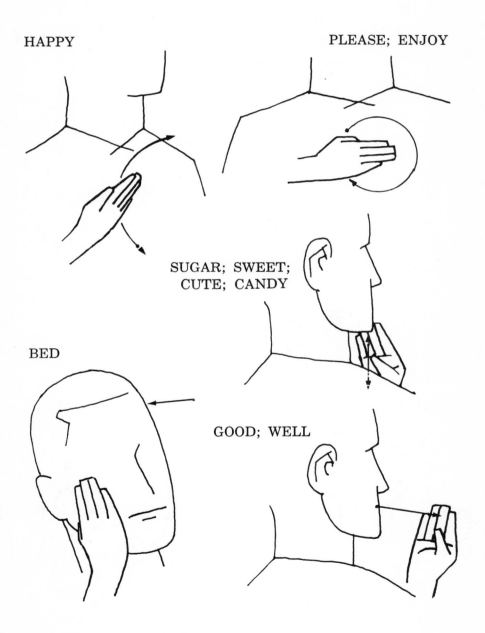

71

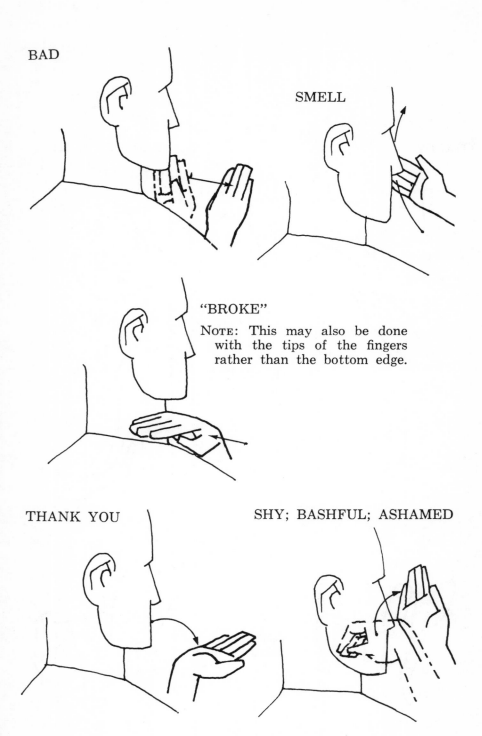

BAD

SMELL

"BROKE"

NOTE: This may also be done with the tips of the fingers rather than the bottom edge.

THANK YOU

SHY; BASHFUL; ASHAMED

Practice:

I am going to bed and sleep 30
   hours.
Are you bashful around girls?
I smell something burning.
Sugar will make you fat.
You sign very well.
Thank you for that excellent
   talk.
What is that bad odor?
I am broke, how about you?
Please don't eat the daisies.
I am happy to tell you that
   you fingerspell well.

HAVE (possess)

WONDERFUL; SUNDAY

AFTER

BEFORE

BABY

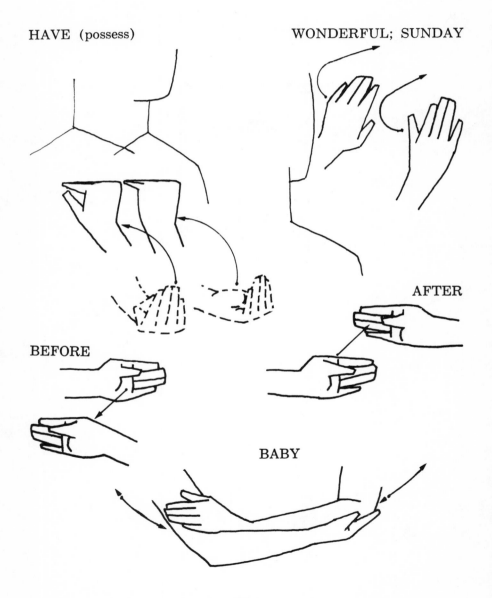

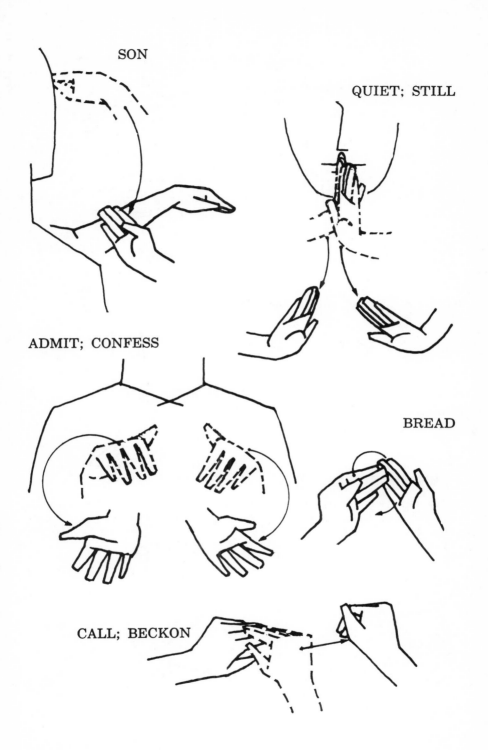

SON

QUIET; STILL

ADMIT; CONFESS

BREAD

CALL; BECKON

75

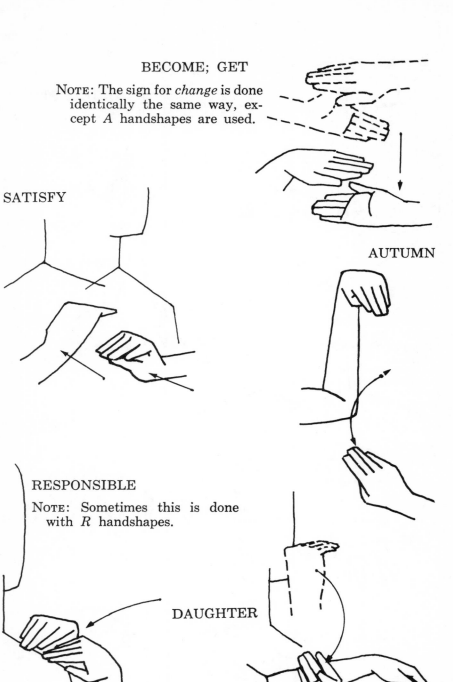

BECOME; GET

NOTE: The sign for *change* is done
identically the same way, except *A* handshapes are used.

SATISFY

AUTUMN

RESPONSIBLE

NOTE: Sometimes this is done
with *R* handshapes.

DAUGHTER

YOUNG

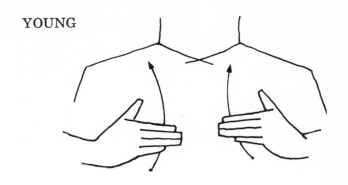

Practice:

I taught school before I came
   here.
Remember all that I taught
   you before you leave.
After this you be more careful.
My son is 4 years old.
My daughter often misunder-
   stands.
When is your birthday?
Schools and colleges open in
   the fall.
You are responsible for your
   own work.
Are you contented with your
   job?
Be still and watch the program.
He admitted all his faults.
You are very young to be in
   college.
Do you have my book?
Are you going to church Sun-
   day?
Who called me?
Do you want bread with your
   cereal?
He left here and became suc-
   cessful.

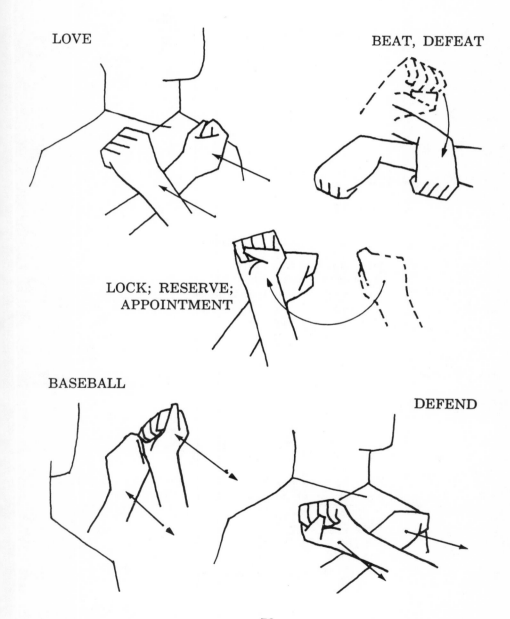

LOVE

BEAT, DEFEAT

LOCK; RESERVE;
APPOINTMENT

BASEBALL

DEFEND

FREE; LIBERTY; SAVE

COFFEE

YEAR

MAKE; FIX

EXAGGERATE; ADVERTISE;
    PROPAGANDIZE

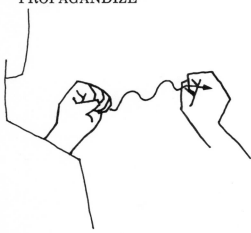

Practice:

Love is truly a beautiful thing.
We must protect our nation.
You will be disappointed if you
    forget to lock it.
Only those who love freedom
    will defend it.
Will you fix it?
Do you like sugar in your
    coffee?
I have been away from home
    11 years.
Baseball is the national sport
    of America.
He always exaggerates when he
    tells something.

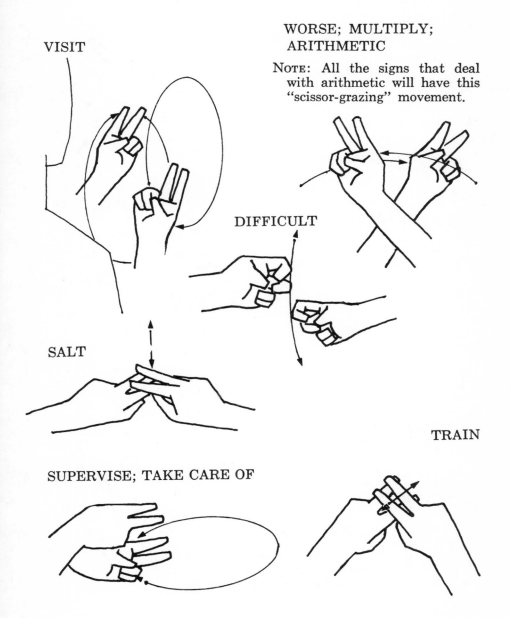

VISIT

WORSE; MULTIPLY;
ARITHMETIC

Note: All the signs that deal
with arithmetic will have this
"scissor-grazing" movement.

DIFFICULT

SALT

TRAIN

SUPERVISE; TAKE CARE OF

SAVE (store away);
RESERVE

KEEP; CAREFUL

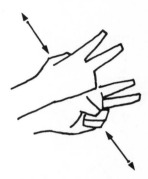

BE CAREFUL; CAREFUL

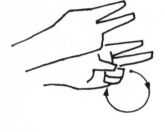

PROBLEM

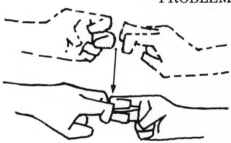

VERY

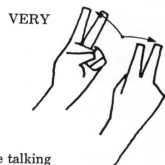

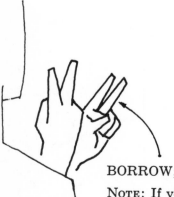

BORROW; LOAN

NOTE: If you yourself are talking
about lending something to
someone, then the movement
is from in-to-out.

SELFISH

NOTE: Sometimes the palms are
up.

HARD

NOTE: Sometimes the left hand
is an *S* handshape, and the
right hand fingers hit the back
of the left hand.

Practice:

I am very tired.
Can you keep a secret?
May I borrow 25 cents?
I loaned him 25 cents yester-
day.
Be careful, don't be careless.
Who is looking after the
children?
Each fall we visit our relatives.
Where is your arithmetic book?
A selfish person has no friends.
Did you come to college on the
train?
The meat needs more salt.
Save some of your money for
emergencies.
It is really hard to compare
individuals.
He is having a difficult time in
college.
The ground is really hard.

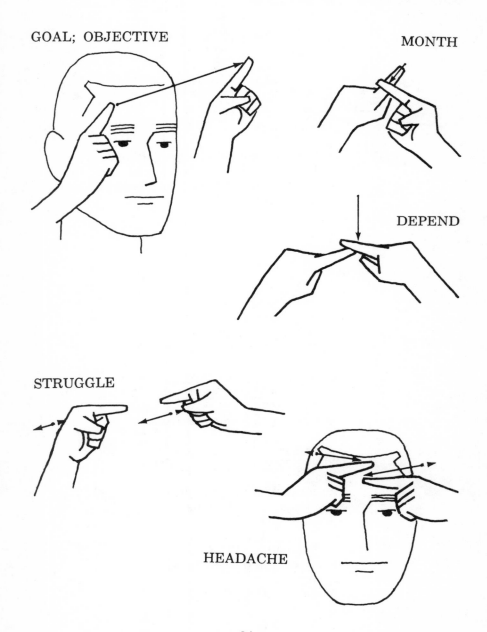

GOAL; OBJECTIVE

MONTH

DEPEND

STRUGGLE

HEADACHE

VARIOUS

NOTE: When the hands move up and down, rather than just wriggling of the fingers, the sign means something more akin to *varies*.

ARGUE; QUARREL

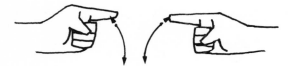

PAIN

NOTE: When the sign is made on parts of the body, it denotes that the pain is there, e.g., *stomachache*.

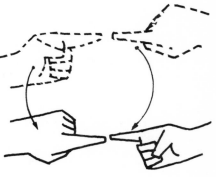

OPPOSITE; DISAGREE

Practice:

The pain is not so bad.
Headaches make me feel cross.
I am depending on you, don't
    disappoint me.
There are various ways to fix
    it.
Each person varies.
Baseball and food seem to be
    his only goals.
What month were you born in?
Brothers and sisters should
    not quarrel.
I have been struggling with
    that a long time.
Good is the opposite of bad.

OBEY; NOTIFY; INFORM

WET

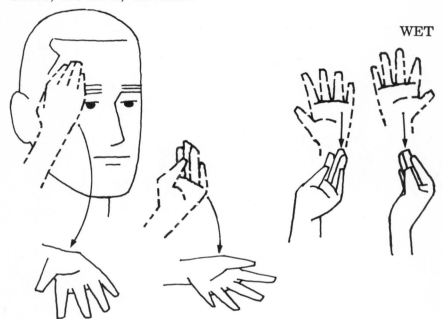

SOFT

OBVIOUS; BRIGHT; CLEAR

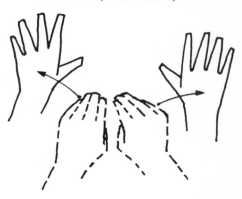

ACCEPT

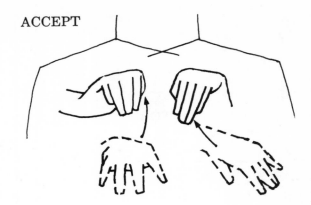

GIVE

NOTE: *Give me* may be done in one sign by beginning farther out and moving in until finger-tips touch chest; keep fingers closed.

CORRESPOND (through letters)

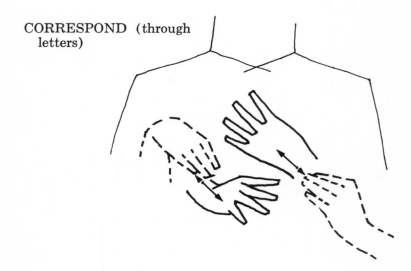

 MEET (congregate)

Practice:

I notified them that we are leaving.

Don't be selfish, give some money.

It is obvious you misunderstood my answer.

Do you write your friends regularly?

You are too soft, you need exercise.

My shoes and coat got wet in the rain.

The students are having a meeting tomorrow.

When you go to college you agree to accept certain responsibilities.

DIE

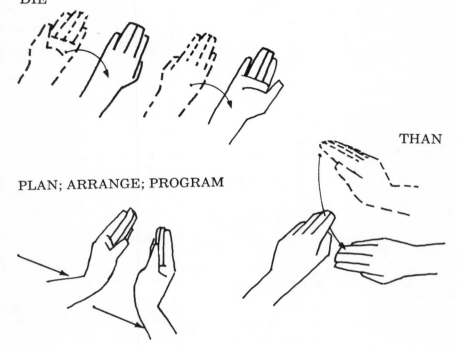

THAN

PLAN; ARRANGE; PROGRAM

FIRE (lose one's job)

ROAD; METHOD; WAY

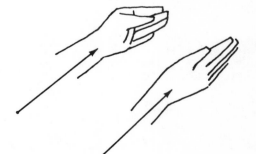

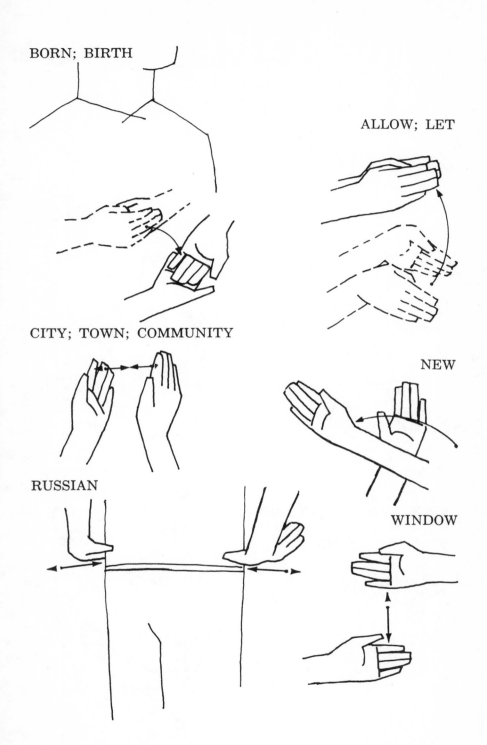

BORN; BIRTH

ALLOW; LET

CITY; TOWN; COMMUNITY

NEW

RUSSIAN

WINDOW

LATE; NOT YET

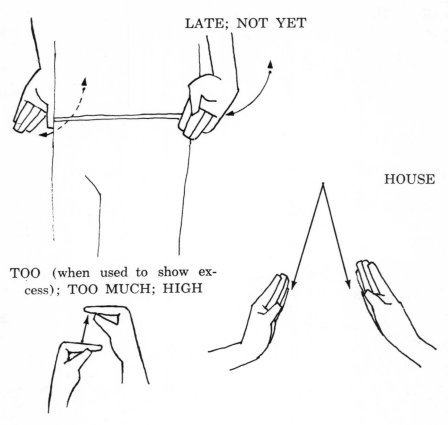

HOUSE

TOO (when used to show excess); TOO MUCH; HIGH

ARRIVE

NOTE: If the right hand is moved slowly toward the left hand, but never actually touches it, this means *approach*.

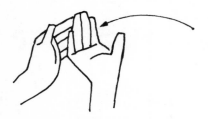

HANDS

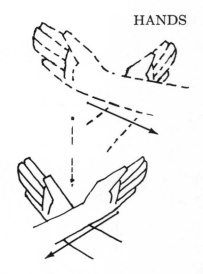

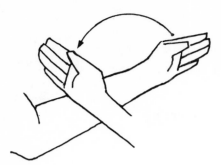

IMPROVE

NOTE: When right hand "bounces" down the left arm, it means *to get worse, regress.*

HAVE (present and past perfect auxiliary); FINISH

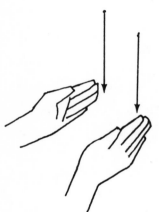

INDIVIDUAL

WORRY; TROUBLE

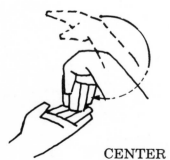

CENTER

Practice:

What <u>month</u> were <u>you</u> born <u>in?</u>
Happy New <u>Year!</u>
<u>I</u> <u>arrived</u> <u>7</u> hours late.
<u>Windows</u> are <u>made</u> of glass.
Enjoy <u>your</u> vacation <u>and</u> don't
   <u>worry</u> so <u>much.</u>
<u>I</u> <u>want</u> a <u>pretty</u> white house.
<u>How</u> far <u>is</u> <u>your</u> <u>home</u> <u>town</u>
   from Washington?
<u>This</u> is the <u>street</u> <u>where</u> <u>my</u>
   <u>house</u> is.
<u>That</u> is <u>not</u> the <u>way</u> to do it.
Children are <u>not</u> permitted to
   <u>sign</u> <u>in</u> a <u>few</u> <u>schools.</u>
If <u>you</u> <u>plan</u> <u>your</u> work <u>you</u> <u>will</u>
   <u>finish</u> it.
<u>Thank</u> the <u>individuals</u> <u>who</u>
   helped <u>you.</u>
<u>I</u> <u>can't</u> <u>fingerspell,</u> <u>my</u> <u>hands</u>
   are <u>too</u> <u>cold.</u>
<u>I</u> <u>have</u> <u>seen;</u> <u>I</u> <u>had</u> <u>eaten;</u> <u>I</u>
   <u>have</u> <u>gone;</u> <u>I</u> <u>had</u> <u>told.</u>
<u>I</u> was <u>fired</u> <u>from</u> <u>my</u> <u>job</u> <u>last</u>
   <u>month.</u>
<u>Has</u> <u>your</u> <u>signing</u> <u>improved</u>
   <u>much?</u>
<u>You</u> <u>eat</u> <u>too</u> <u>much.</u>
He <u>eats</u> faster <u>than</u> <u>I</u> <u>do.</u>
<u>I</u> <u>haven't</u> <u>eaten</u> yet. (Common
   usage says: "<u>I</u> <u>late</u> <u>eat.</u>")
Do <u>you</u> <u>speak</u> <u>Russian?</u>

SICK
NOTE: Often the left hand is
also placed on the stomach.

HATE

FEEL; EMOTION

DIRTY

TASTE

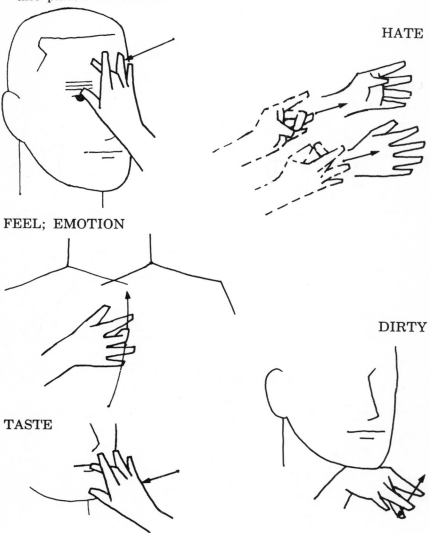

THRILL; EXCITE

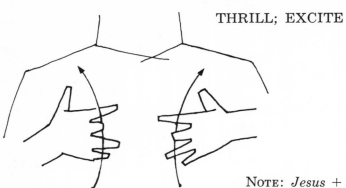

JESUS

NOTE: *Jesus + book = Bible*

INTELLIGENT; SMART

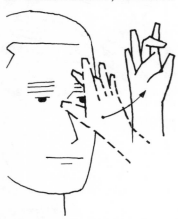

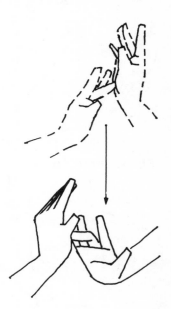

LIKE; INTEREST; INTERESTING

NOTE: Often done with both hands.

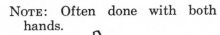

Practice:

He was very sick.

He is truly brilliant, but he doesn't have enough patience.

Every time I taste castor oil, I get sick.

Can you wash my dirty socks with yours?

I feel silly because of how I acted.

I don't like snow when it's melting.

Jesus taught that you should be kind to all people.

I hate people who don't agree with me.

The students were all excited over the victory.

ODD; QUEER

HUNT; SEARCH; LOOK FOR

HUNGRY; WISH

MARRY

LISTEN

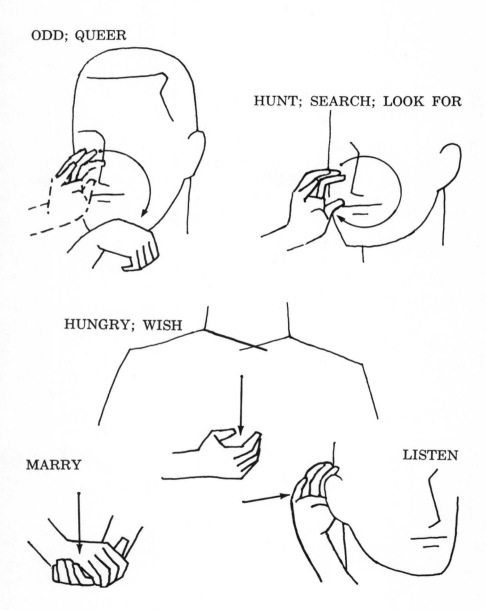

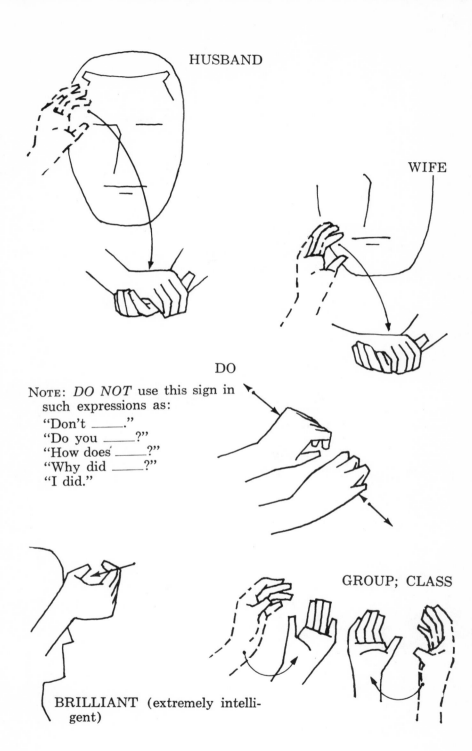

HUSBAND

WIFE

DO

NOTE: *DO NOT* use this sign in
such expressions as:
"Don't _____."
"Do you _____?"
"How does _____?"
"Why did _____?"
"I did."

GROUP; CLASS

BRILLIANT (extremely intelligent)

Practice:

He is brilliant in algebra.
The story seemed a little odd
   to me.
We looked for you but you
   were gone.
Listen and you will hear.
I am so hungry I could eat a
   horse.
A happy marriage is based on
   love.
A good husband plans in
   advance.
A good wife makes her hus-
   band happy.
Do you plan to join a club?
What are you doing?

ITALY; ITALIAN

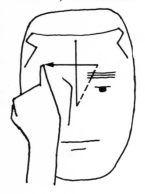

INSTITUTION;
RESIDENTIAL SCHOOL

NOTE: This sign is often used in the phrase *school for the deaf* to distinguish it from day schools. It is, however, being discouraged in favor of the sign *school.*

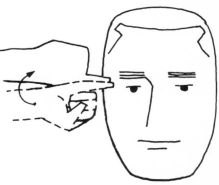

IDEA; IMAGINE

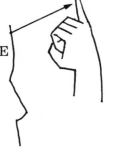

LAST (in line, etc.)

NOTE: This may also be done with the right hand in the *1* handshape.

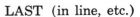

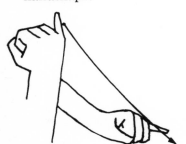

JAPAN; JAPANESE

Practice:

I have no idea why.
My uncle came from Italy in 1921.
I would really feel bad if that happened to me.
Japan is a very industrious country.
I am last in line almost every day.
I attended a residential school for 13 years.

LOAF; VACATION

MONDAY

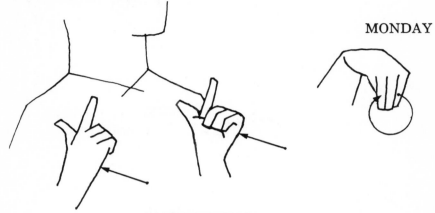

MATHEMATICS

PEOPLE

DOCTOR

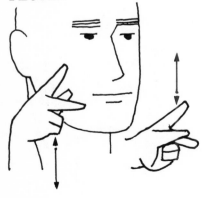

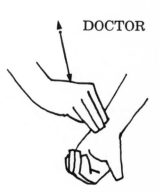

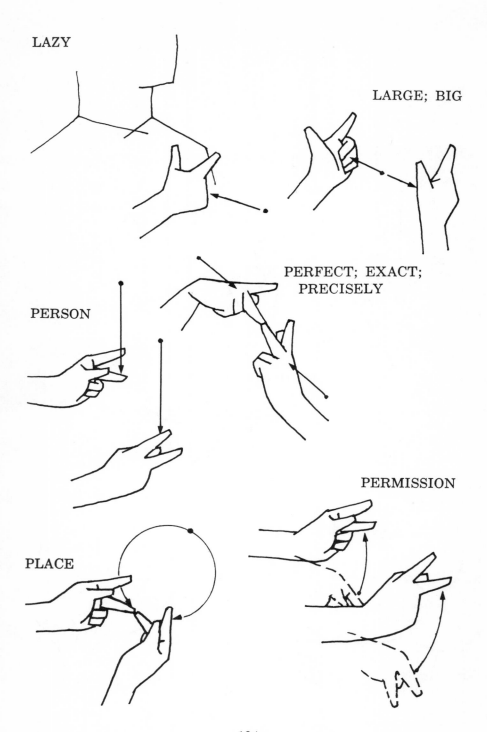

LAZY

LARGE; BIG

PERFECT; EXACT;
PRECISELY

PERSON

PERMISSION

PLACE

104

Practice:

He <u>won't</u> <u>work</u> <u>because</u> he is <u>lazy</u>.

<u>Have</u> <u>you</u> been <u>loafing</u>?

<u>Are</u> you <u>sure</u> <u>you</u> <u>want</u> a <u>big</u> <u>house</u>?

<u>My</u> <u>doctor</u> <u>told</u> <u>me</u> to get <u>lots</u> of <u>sleep</u>.

<u>I</u> <u>told</u> her to <u>come</u> <u>on</u> Monday.

If <u>you</u> are <u>not</u> <u>good</u> <u>in</u> <u>math</u>, <u>don't</u> take physics.

<u>I</u> want a <u>person</u> <u>who</u> <u>will</u> be <u>happy</u>.

Many <u>queer</u> <u>people</u> are <u>really</u> <u>smart</u>.

Did <u>you</u> get <u>permission</u> to <u>talk</u>?

<u>That's</u> the <u>place</u> <u>where</u> <u>I</u> left it.

<u>No</u> <u>one</u> is perfect.

105

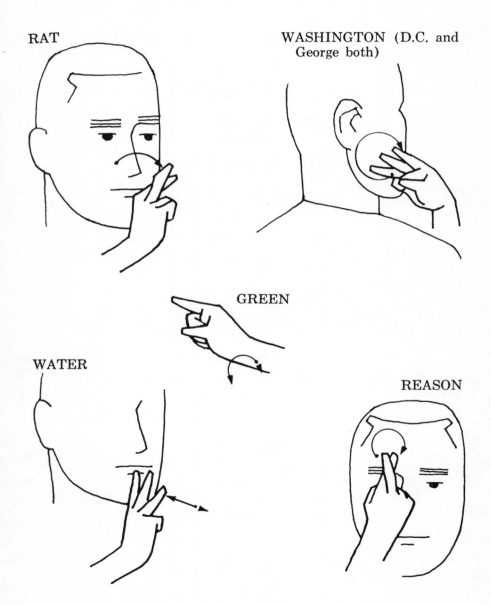

RAT

WASHINGTON (D.C. and George both)

GREEN

WATER

REASON

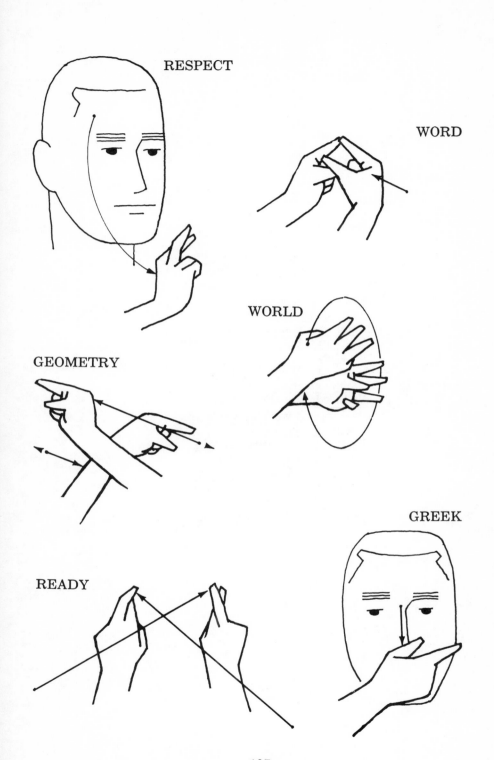

RESPECT

WORD

WORLD

GEOMETRY

GREEK

READY

107

Practice:

That is the reason why I won't
go.
College students often have
difficult financial problems.
He has no respect for learning.
Some students are not ready
to accept that idea.
I can see you Tuesday.
You can't bathe in that dirty
water.
A visit to Washington can be
very exciting.
Wednesday is the last day.
She stopped working while you
were in school.
We live in a confused world.
I don't like green apples.
He studied Greek in college.
Geometry is truly a difficult
subject for some.
The Greeks had a word for it.

HOPE; EXPECT

DISAPPEAR

NOTE: Reverse the movement of this sign and you have *appear*, or *show up*.

BEGIN; START

DEAF

NEXT WEEK

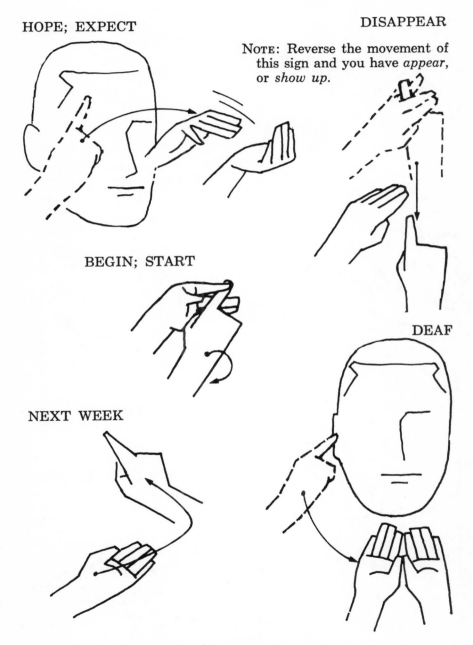

SHOW; DEMONSTRATE;
ILLUSTRATE; EXAMPLE

PAY

ONCE

NOTE: If movement is repeated
2–3 times, it means *sometimes*.

DEBT; OWE

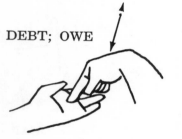

LAST WEEK

MAJOR SUBJECT; LINE OF
WORK

PROMISE

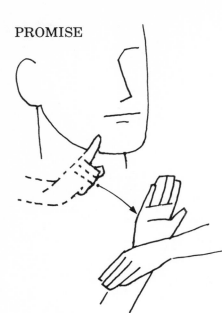

WEEK

NOTE: When movement is repeated 2–3 times, it means
"weekly."

TALL

DISCUSS; DEBATE;
ARGUMENT

NOTE: This sign may be used for
argue, argument only when it
is meant argue as in a debate.
If *quarrel* is meant, use the
sign on p. 85.

CRITICIZE; CORRECT (as in
correcting exams); CANCEL

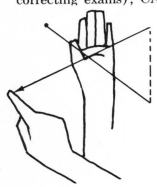

PRAISE;
CONGRATULATIONS

111

Practice:

I hope you won't be dis-
appointed.
My brother is deaf.
Promise me that you will wait.
Congratulations, you won!
How tall are you?
I enjoy listening to debates.
There are about 4 weeks in a
    month.
My father will come next week.
I enjoyed a good movie last
    week.
He was famous for a long time
    and then he just disappeared.
Show me where you hunted.
He owes me a lot.
She told me once, but I have.
    forgotten.
Have you paid for your clothes?
Have you started working yet?
I hope he grades my test soon.
What is your line of work?

BELIEVE

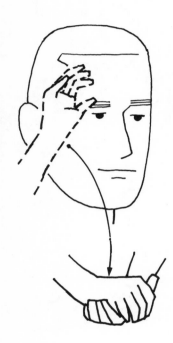

GUESS

CONDENSE; ABBREVIATE

ENGLISH; ENGLAND

CHURCH

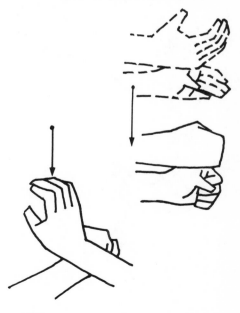

OLD; AGE

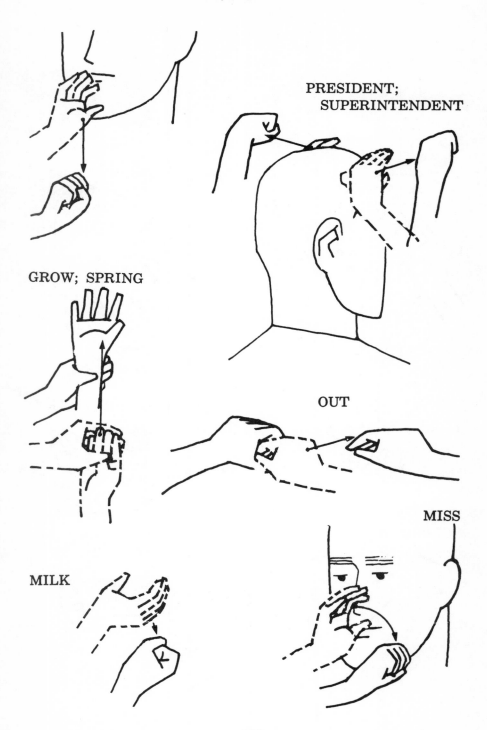

PRESIDENT;
SUPERINTENDENT

GROW; SPRING

OUT

MISS

MILK

Practice:

I guess that's right.
I missed that movie.
How old are you?
Do you like cream in your
  cereal?
Our president lives under ter-
  rific pressure.
Your paper was lengthy, con-
  dense it.
What church do you attend?
You must watch your English.
  (NOTE: "Watch" here is
  signed "be careful.")
Do you believe me?
In the Spring, everything is
  fresh.
How do you get out of here?

LESSON 35

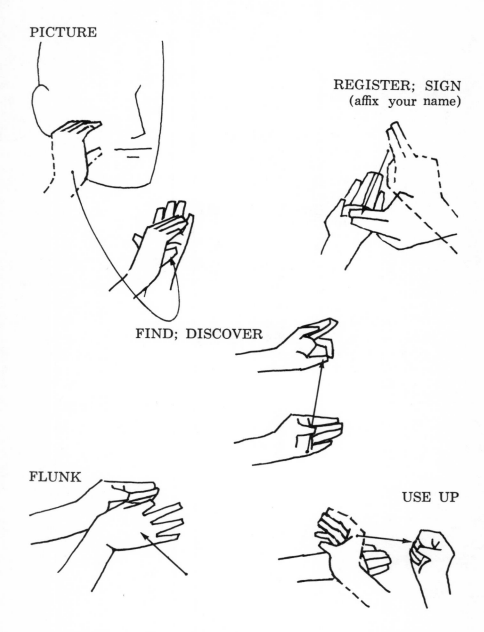

PICTURE

REGISTER; SIGN
(affix your name)

FIND; DISCOVER

FLUNK

USE UP

116

EARN

COUNT

MEAT

DUTY

MAGAZINE

GRADUATE

HONEST

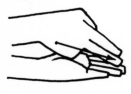

Practice:

Where is your picture?
Will you earn enough to pay
your debts?
Is the food gone (used up)?
Deaf college graduates owe a
duty to deaf people.
Columbus discovered America
in 1492.
He flunked because he loafed
too much.
Count all the people, please.
Go get good, red meat.
What magazine are you read-
ing?
We will graduate in 1966.
Have you finished registering?
Be honest in your work.

BETTER

BEST

WITHOUT

IMPRESS; EMPHASIZE

ESTABLISH

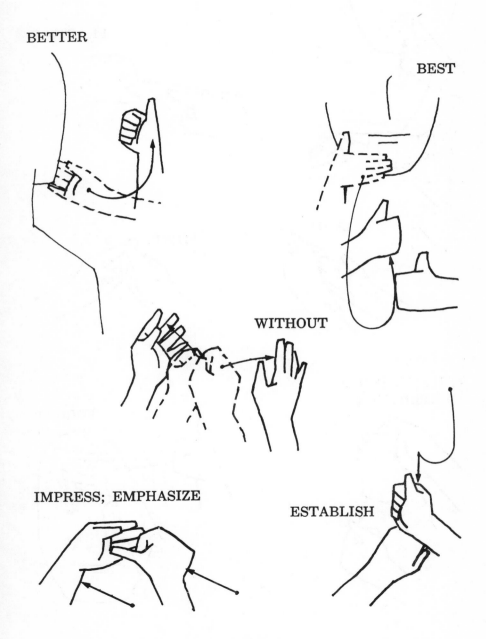

LETTER; MAIL

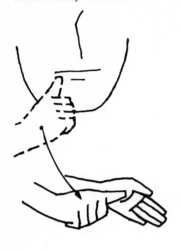

PRACTICE

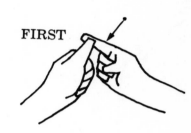

LEAD

FIRST

ABILITY; SKILL; EXPERTNESS

FORGET

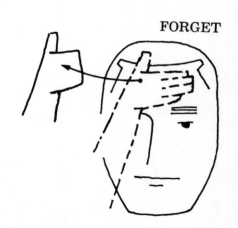

Practice:

I liked the book better.
Do your best and try.
Who can lead us?
He is very skilled in algebra.
When was Gallaudet College
    established?
His brilliance impressed me.
Did I get some mail yesterday?
I forgot my lesson for today.
How often do you practice?
To lead, you must first learn to
    follow.
You can't succeed without
    practice.

MEMORIZE

NOTE: Often this sign starts with a 5 handshape, rather than the B handshape for *know*. Movement is the same.

STUDY

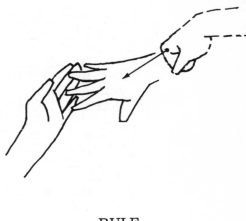

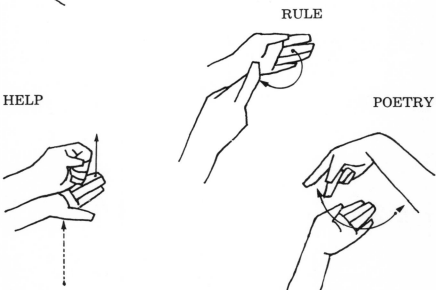

RULE

HELP

POETRY

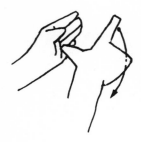

LATER; AFTERWHILE; "IN A MINUTE"; AWHILE

NOTE: Do not confuse this with *late* (p. 92). This *later* denotes the passing of time or a specific amount of time. *Late* denotes a state of being.

ENOUGH; PLENTY

FILL

DRAW

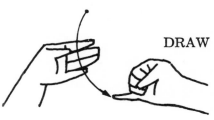

LAW

NOTE: When this movement is vigorous, the sign means that something is *prohibited, illegal, against the law.*

Practice:

He draws pretty pictures.
I will finish it later.
The law says you must pay.
Do you enjoy poetry?
We need to make a new rule.
The class is full, come back
later.
There is enough food for one
week.
Will you help me with my
math?
Seems to me he doesn't want
to study.
Try to memorize some more
poetry.

FRENCH

NOTE: Also can be done with the movement out.

SPIRIT; SOUL

IMPORTANT

JOIN

TEA

EXPLAIN; DESCRIBE

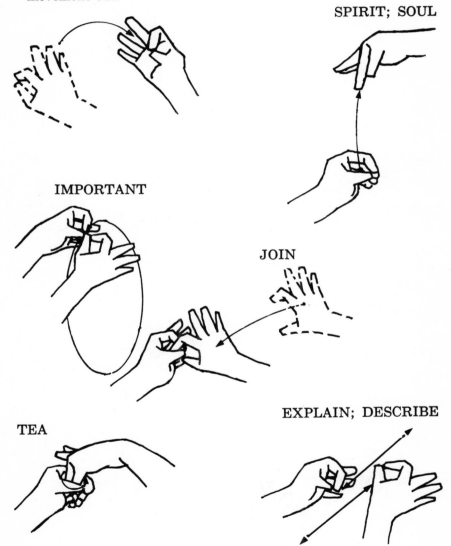

AWFUL; TERRIBLE

NOTE: *Awful* is also often made with an *O* handshape instead of the *F*. The movement is the same, all fingers open up.

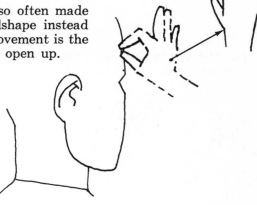

INSTEAD OF

LANGUAGE; SENTENCE

INTERESTING

EXCEPT

126

VOLUNTEER; CANDIDATE;
  APPLY

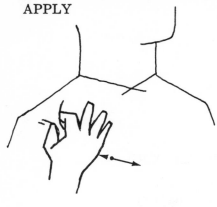

VOTE; ELECT

CURIOUS

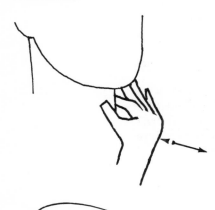

DECIDE

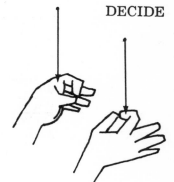

COOPERATE

NOTE: When the movement is in and out or left and right, it means *related*, *connected*, *associated*, etc.

Practice:

I am curious to see your
answer.
I volunteered to lead them.
We are leaving for Canada on
Friday.
He is very skilled in French.
That is an awful mess.
When did you decide to leave?
How do you explain this error?
If it is important to you then
work hard.
Watch your language! (*Watch*
comes from *be careful.*)
Can you join our group?
When we cooperate our work is
easy.
Your paper was very inter-
esting.
Whom did you vote for?
Where is your college spirit?
Do you like lemon in your tea?
All but one came. (NOTE: Here
but means *except.*)

LESSON 39

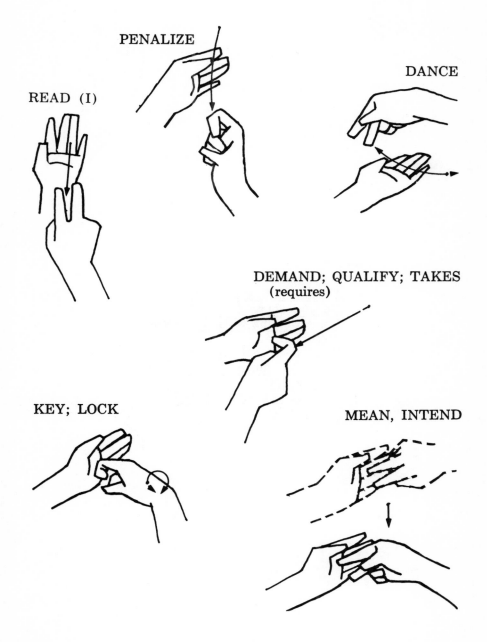

PENALIZE

READ (I)

DANCE

DEMAND; QUALIFY; TAKES
(requires)

KEY; LOCK

MEAN, INTEND

STAND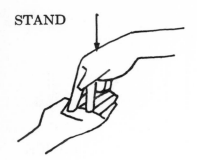

READ (II)

NOTE: It is optional which *read* you use.

Practice:

I stood and waited for 2 hours.
Do you enjoy dancing?
I was running when I slipped-and-fell.
What does that sign mean?
Did you finish reading the newspaper?
It takes 124 hours of study to graduate.
I can't find my key.
If you disregard the law, you will be fined.

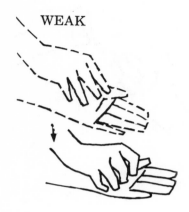

WEAK

LEARN

COPY; IMITATE

NOTE: The movement may be in
various directions: in, out, side-
ways, etc. When it moves out,
it means *copy me* or *follow me*,
or *imitate me*.

TELEGRAM

MEDICINE

WRITE; PENCIL

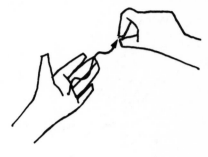

MOVIE

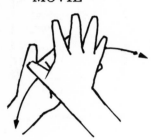

Practice:

Copy the paper carefully.
Are you here to learn or to play?
After all that exercise, I am weak.
What kind of movie do you like best?
Sunday morning I got a telegram from her.
I hate to take medicine.
May I borrow your pencil?

LESSON 41

STUPID

GIVE UP

NEXT YEAR

TOUCH

WIN

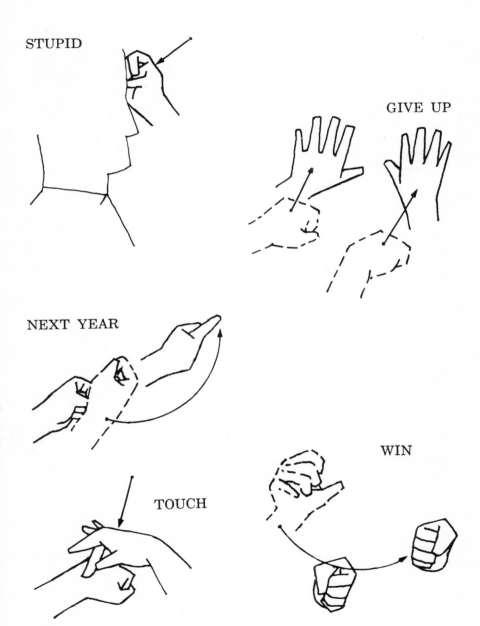

LAST YEAR

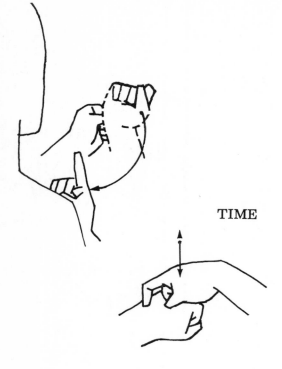

GERMAN

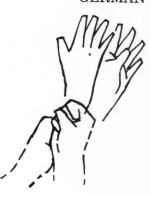

TIME

COUNSEL, ADVISE

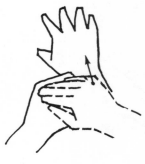

TAKE; TAKE UP

BEAT, DEFEAT

POTATO; IRISH

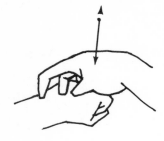

GET, RECEIVE

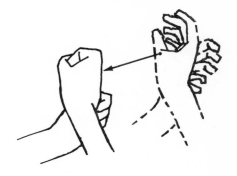

DROP

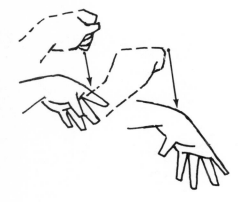

EARTH; GEOGRAPHY

VACANT, EMPTY

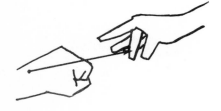

YES

Practice:

Why do people do such stupid
  things!
Yes, I know.
Our football team beat theirs.
I want potatoes, please.
What time will you meet us?
Next year we will go to Russia
  on our vacation.
Last year I flunked math.
When you must, don't be
  afraid to go to the Counsel-
  ing Center.
Did you get enough sleep?
You must sacrifice a lot if you
  want to win.
Do you read German?
Did you drop Russian last
  year?
Do you plan to take German?
Don't give up, you can finish.
The earth is round like a ball.
Don't touch that wet paint.
Is that house vacant?

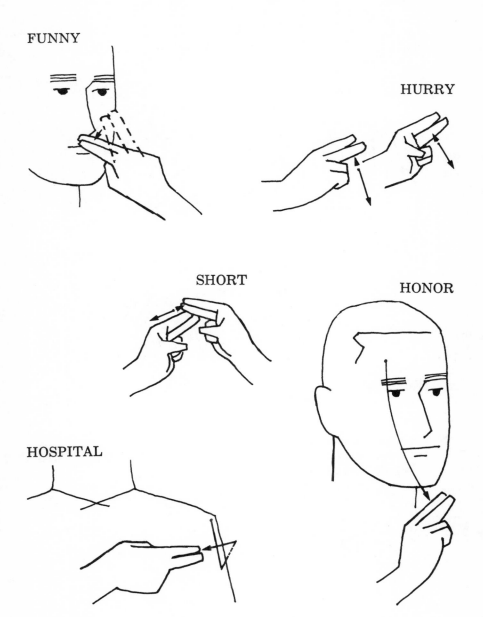

FUNNY

HURRY

SHORT

HONOR

HOSPITAL

QUIT

NOTE: *Participate* has the opposite movement, that is, insert the fingers into the *O*.

CATHOLIC

EGG

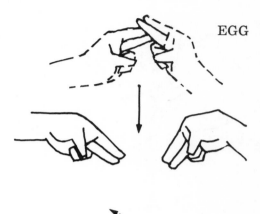

WEIGHT; POUNDS

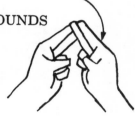

NAME

NOTE: Use this sign in such sentences as, "I *called* him 'Bob'," "What do you *call* it?"

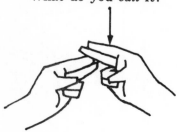

SIT; SEAT; CHAIR

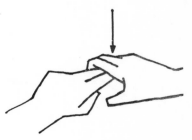

HISTORY

USE

Practice:

Do you belong to the Catholic
Church? (Sign *belong to* as
joined with.)

Can you read Latin?

I feel funny when you stare at
me. (*Stare at me* is done all
in one sign. Just reverse *look*
so that your fingers point at
you. The movement up and
down is comparable to the
expression, "Look me over.")

When you are very ill, go to
the hospital.

I like to use the train instead
of driving.

Do you like American History?

I was impressed by his accept-
ing the honor with humility.

I was in such a hurry I almost
didn't bring my books.

What is your last name?

That was a short meeting.

He weighs about 101 pounds.
(Do not sign *pounds*, it is
implied in the sign, *weigh*.)

Why did you quit school?

Don't sit on the wet ground.

SPANISH

MUST, SHOULD, OUGHT, SUPPOSED TO; NEED, NECESSARY

GIVE

TEASE; HAZE; DAMAGE, RUIN

TEST

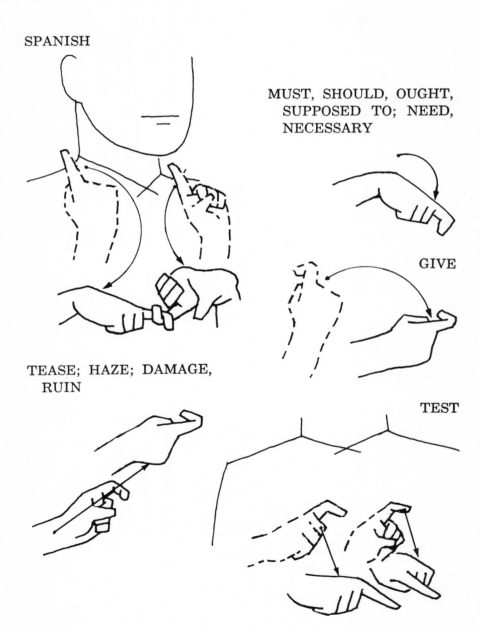

ASK (a question)

DRY; DULL, BORING

SUMMER

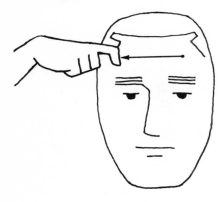

FRIEND

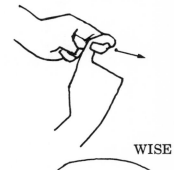

PHYSICS; ELECTRICITY

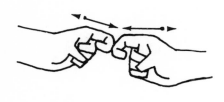

WISE

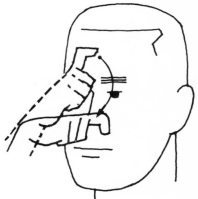

141

UGLY

Practice:

Do you think that is wise?
I am lazy during the summer.
Many beautiful personalities
   are hidden by ugly faces.
   (Sign *looks* for *faces*.)
He sure gave a dull speech.
You have to go.
I gave him my candy.
I asked him if he was "broke."
You will ruin it if you give up
   so easily.
You should be good in math if
   you plan to take physics.
I always depend on my friends
   to help me when I need
   them.
I will take Spanish.
Did you take the test last
   week?

SHAVE

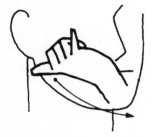

STILL, CONTINUE,
ENDURE, LAST

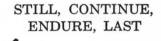

WRONG, MISTAKE

SILLY, FOOL, RIDICULOUS

TELEPHONE

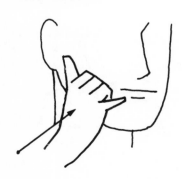

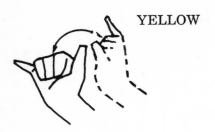

YELLOW

FLY (in an airplane)

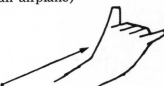

STAY

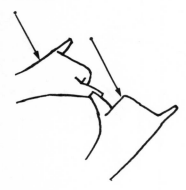

PLAY

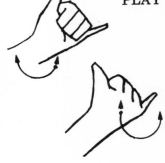

SAME (usually used when com-
paring things)

CIGARETTE

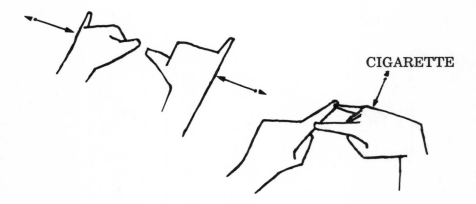

Practice:

Most men shave everyday.
Can you use the telephone?
Learn to accept criticism when
 you are wrong.
It would be foolish to quit now.
She has beautiful blond hair.
    (For *hair*, just pinch a few
    strands of your hair.)
Did you fly to Washington?
Do you still go to the movies
 every Saturday?
Can't you stay until I leave?
I have the same problem.
He likes to play games.
We have many students from
 California.
Lend me a cigarette.

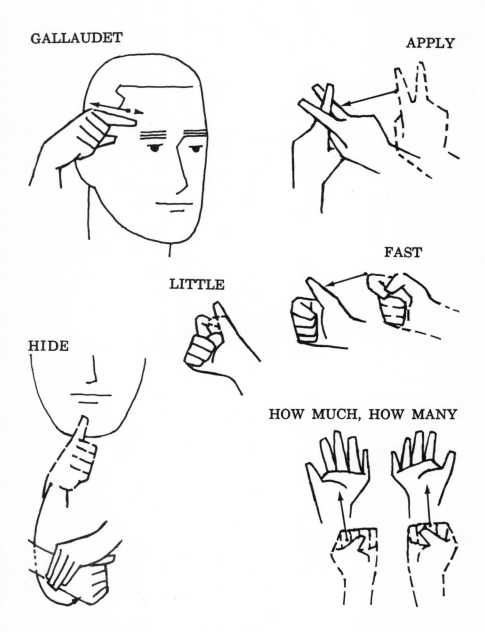

GALLAUDET

APPLY

FAST

LITTLE

HIDE

HOW MUCH, HOW MANY

GOSSIP

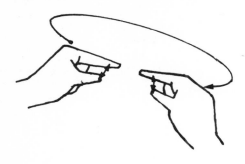

BOTH

REVENGE

NOTE: If the movement is reversed, that is the lower hand is stationary and the upper hand moves down more slowly, it means *exact*.

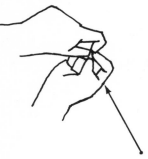

MANY

SURPRISE; AWAKE, WAKE UP

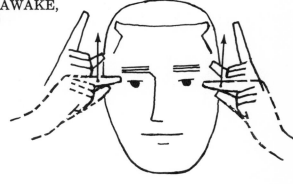

Practice:

Give me a little sugar, please.
You eat too fast.
I am going to Gallaudet next year.
Gossip has ruined many good people.
I am surprised that you understand so well.
He is always looking for revenge.
I enjoy riding streetcars.
Many of my friends are gone.
How many do you want?
Both boys have improved a lot.
Have you applied for work?

In order to convey the idea of a person doing some act, a "suffix" sign is used. If, for example, you wanted to say "teacher," you would make first the sign for "teach," then follow it immediately with the "suffix." This changes the "teach" to "teacher." Practice converting these words yourself:

believer	salesman
counselor	student
leader	member
speaker	actor
loser	critic
receiver	applicant
visitor	poet
worker	guard
player	opponent
dancer	pilot
supervisor	debater
scientist	

There are many shortcuts in signing and fingerspelling. We cannot practically list all of them. You will discover them as you gain experience. In fingerspelling, they usually take the form of abbreviating long words. "Pennsylvania" becomes "Pa" or "Penn," "Vocational Rehabilitation" becomes "Voc Rehab" and so on.

In signing, these short cuts take the form of making the sign with only one hand, shortening the movement and changing the place where the sign occurs. Much of this "abbreviating" takes place in a relaxed atmosphere, particularly when sitting. When there is a table near, or even the arm of a chair, you will see the table top or chair arm become the "other hand."

Almost every locality will have certain signs that are known only in that locality. You have to learn these by contact with the deaf people in that area. These usually consist of names of people, cities, important places and often just words have different signs.

It is appropriate that we close these lessons with a few pointers on etiquette.

Never interrupt a conversation, this is rude and annoys deaf people as much as it does hearing people. This is most flagrantly committed when a deaf person and a hearing person are conversing. Up walks a hearing person and starts speaking orally with the other hearing person. If you happen to be the hearing person talking with the deaf person, just hold your finger up towards the hearing person who is interrupting. This should cue him to shut up and wait until you turn and show him that you are ready to listen. Above all, keep your eyes on the deaf person and make it obvious to the hearing person that he does not have your attention.

Don't get in the midst of a conversation. This often happens in a room with many conversations going on. Before you stand still or sit down, check to be sure you aren't blocking someone's view.

Deaf people are hypersensitive to vibrations. Don't stamp your feet unnecessarily, tap your toe on a chair, drum your fingers on a table. A deaf person is conditioned to respond to a vibration by turning and facing it. In fact, to get their attention, one stamp on the floor will usually do it. So it can be seen that an unnecessary stamp can interrupt many conversations.

Usually a gentle tap on the arm or shoulder is sufficient to get a deaf person's attention. Never grab them by the arm or pull on their clothing except in emergencies.

A SIGN-LANGUAGE BIBLIOGRAPHY

Bayne, H. L., *Basic Signs* (No publisher—one pamphlet in Gallaudet Library.)

Becker, Valentine A. *Underwater Sign Language*, Catalog No. 1919 U. S. Divers Corps. (Write to author, Supervisor of Physically Handicapped, Public School System, San Francisco, California.)

Benson, Elizabeth, *Suggestions Relative to the Mastery of the Language of Signs*. (An unpublished manual used in teaching sign language at Gallaudet College.)

* Cissna, Roy L. *Introduction to the Sign Language*, Jefferson City, Missouri: Missouri Baptist Convention, Baptist Building (no date.)

DeLaney, Theo. *Sing Unto the Lord, a hymnal for the deaf.* Ephphetha Conference of Lutheran Pastors for the Deaf, 1959. (Songs are translated into signs.)

* Falberg, Roger M., *The Language of Silence*, Wichita Social Services for the Deaf, Wichita, Kansas: 1962.

Fauth, Bette La Verne and Fauth, Warren Wesley, "A Study of Proceedings of the Convention of American Instructors of the Deaf 1850-1949, IV," Chapter XIII, "The Manual Alphabet," *American Annals of the Deaf*, 96:292–296, March 1951. (Bibliography included.)

Fauth, Bette La Verne and Fauth, Warren Wesley, "Sign Language," *American Annals of the Deaf*, 100:253–263, March 1955.

Higgins, Daniel D., C.S.S.R., *How to Talk to the Deaf*, Mount Carmel Guild, Archdiocese of Newark, 1959. Distributed by Archdiocesan Audio-Visual, Archdiocese of Newark, N.J.

Jordan, Florence. *Lesson Outlines for Teaching and the Study of Dactylology*. Christian Deaf Fellowship, 75 Brodgen Lane, Hampton, Va.

Long, J. Schuyler, *The Sign Language*, A Manual of Signs, Washington, D.C.: Gallaudet College, 1962 reprint of second edition.

Michaels, J. W. *A Handbook of the Sign Language*, Atlanta: Home Mission Board Southern Baptist Convention, 1923.

Peet, Elizabeth, "The Philology of the Sign Language," (reprint) *Buff and Blue*, Gallaudet College, March, 1921.

* Riekehof, Lottie L., *Talk To The Deaf*, Gospel Publishing House, 1445 Boonville Ave., Springfield, Missouri.

Roth, Stanley D. *A Basic Book of Signs Used by the Deaf*, Fulton, Missouri: Missouri School for the Deaf, 1948.

* Springer, C. S., C.S.S.R. *Talking with the Deaf*, Redemptorist Fathers, 5354 Plank Rd., Baton Rouge, La., 1961

* Stokoe, W. C. *Sign Language Structure: An Outline of the Visual Communication Systems of the American Deaf*, Buffalo 14: University of Buffalo, Dept. of Anthropology and Linguistics. (Studies in Linguistics, Occasional Papers 8, 1960.) Write to author, Gallaudet College, Washington 2, D.C.

* Watson, David, *Talk With Your Hands*, Winneconne, Wisconsin.

* Wisher, Peter R. *Use of the Sign Language in Underwater Communication*.

152

The following indexes to the *American Annals of the Deaf* indicate additional references to articles in the *Annals* that deal with sign language. The page numbers given refer to the pages in the indexes on which these articles are listed.

INDEX NO.	PAGE NO.	INDEX NO.	PAGE NO.
I	40–45	VI	433
II	85–87	VII	537–538
III	86	VIII	545
IV	75	IX	404
V	78		

* Books that are asterisked may also be purchased from the Gallaudet College Bookstore, Gallaudet College, Washington, D. C. 20002.

INDEX OF SIGNS
(Alphabetically)

Word	Page	Word	Page